All first names given in the examples and incidents are changed.

When we speak of God in this book, we speak of God the Father, the father of Jesus, "Abba", as Jesus calls him.

When we speak of Jesus, we speak of Jesus Christ, the Son of the Father.

When we speak of the Holy Spirit, we speak of the Spirit whom Jesus has sent us as our helper and advocate.

All given bible quotes are taken from the bible translation of the "New International Version (NIV)".

Heinrich and Hildegard Becker

About Hearing

Praying, Blessing, Counselling

© 2013 Heinrich and Hildegard Becker

Illustration: H. Becker

Original Title: Vom Hören

Translation from German to English: Kerstin Becker and Susan Schuelke

Production and publisher:
BoD – Books on Demand, Norderstedt/Germany

ISBN:978-3-7322-4713-4

Table of Contents:

Preface	7
Introduction	11
About Hearing	24
Forgiveness	57
Starting Points	71
Practical Tips and Tools	89
Incidents	128
Epilogue	151

Preface

God knows us, God knows you!

That sounds trivial – at first. But when I bring to my mind that I personally know who the President of the Unites States is and that I know him or her, but he or she does not even know of my existence, then this statement gains significant value. When I furthermore envision that God so loves me that he knows countless details of my life, then this shall open my eyes for God's interest in me. God the Father has billions of children, but he knows each one individually and personally. Moreover, God has chosen us before he created the world[1], he has pondered over us for uncountable years, and he now wants to speak to us about what he has placed within us. All of our lifetime will not suffice therefor, as we shall see.

Unfortunately, a lot has gone wrong in our lives to this day. People have become guilty towards us, and we have become guilty towards them.

---

[1] Ephesians 1:3-4 and similar in Jeremiah 1:4

God knows you!

This statement can unfortunately make me believe that God has a long list with all my faults, my failures and my guilt; and that he catches me every time I do something wrong or when I have a bad day. And this list gets longer and longer every day.

But this is not the case! In the Gospel according to Luke[2] Jesus tells us about his Father in the parable of the prodigal son. The strangest moment is when the son arrives at his father's house, after his return – and the father does not accuse or settle up with him, but starts with the restoration of the son into his original status, without properly listening to the son's confession. He tells him: "It is great that you are here again." And he does not leave him in the olds rags in which he came, symbolising his slave status. He neither gives him the status of a hireling nor of a foreman nor of a servant such as Eliezer of Damascus[3] who will inherit the estate if no heir is born. No, the father reinstates him into the status of a son, without any contribution from the prodigal son's side.

Jesus says: This is how the Father is like. He is a Father who has time for me (!). He is not interested in my guilt, but in my trust in him. By the way, fatherhood (and motherhood) are the only "contracts" that

---

[2] Luke 15:11-31
[3] Genesis 15:2

are irredeemable. Marriages can be divorced, work contracts can be rescinded, and purchase contracts can be revoked. But parenthood cannot be rescinded. Parents can decide whether they want to have a child or not, but once the child is born they will "forever" remain father and mother to this child. How much more does this apply to God, the Father, who has wanted us ever since the creation of the world?

God knows you!

You know God, but he knows you better than you can imagine. Let us read Isaiah 43:1 et seqq. and let us replace the names of Jacob or Israel with our own names.

Verse 1: "But now, this is what the Lord says— he who created you, Jacob, he who formed you, Israel: 'Do not fear, for I have redeemed you; I have summoned you by name; you are mine.' "

Verse 5: "Do not be afraid, for I am with you; I will bring your children from the east and gather you from the west."

Verse 6: "I will say to the north, 'Give them up!' and to the south, 'Do not hold them back.' Bring my sons from afar and my daughters from the ends of the earth."

God knows you!

This book tells about the experiences we have made with hearing prayer, hearing blessings and hearing counselling. The most astonishing fact first: Whenever we had time to listen to God, the Holy Spirit also had time for us. It is just as Moses experienced it: As soon as he entered the tent of meeting, God came to meet him in the pillar of cloud.[4]

God's interest with his people and with every single one of us has always been to reinstate us into the life with him that he had initially planned for us. And God always acts individually with each of his children, he never acts the same, he does not use methods.

It is an honour for us to be present when God acts and gets involved with people. Would you like to be "infected" with God's love and acting?

---

[4] Exodus 33:9

Introduction

It is helpful to start with a definition what counselling is and what it is not. In her book, Martina Plieth[5] explains the different scientific forms of psychology:

"Psychology is the science that examines the conscious processes and conditions as well as their causes and effects.[6] It is the science of subjective life processes that are linked with objective ones.

Depth psychology is understood as a collective term for the subdivision of psychology that claims not to stick to the surface of the conscious soul life, but to penetrate into the subconscious and unconscious depth of the soul and thereby to put forward the "instinct-dynamic" relationship between one's will and emotions. An exact definition of the term "depth psychology" is very complex because – as F. Dorsch rightly remarks – depth psychology has become **science, therapy and philosophy** at once.

Psychoanalysis can be understood as a "treatment originally developed at the end of the 19th century by Breuer and Freud to cure psychological illnesses" and can, if developed into depth psychology science, be

---

[5] Martina Plieth, Die Seele wahrnehmen (Perceiving one's soul), Publisher: Vandenhoeck & Ruprecht (1994)
[6] (Rohracher) Dorsch 1976, Psychologisches Wörterbuch 9th edition, page 465

categorized as part of the latter.

Psychotherapy shall be understood as the science of the treatment of psychological and psychologically induced illnesses with the help of psychological means.

What **counselling** means in its entity is not easy to determine and can only be defined with the help of examples. "

How can we perform counselling when God never does the same thing twice? When Jesus never performed the same miracle twice? Even his healings differed from each other and were individually tailored to the people concerned.
The answer is: There is no method. Just like Martina Plieth suggested, this book is an exemplary attempt to contemplate and to describe the essence of counselling from another point of view. Here is an observation that we have made in churches and in Christian environments:

- It is wrong to believe that forgiveness and healing from wounds will just happen by itself when someone has decided to give his/her life to Jesus. That is not the case, as we can read in 2 Corinthians 5:17: "Therefore, if anyone is in Christ, the new creation has come: The old has gone, the new is here!" Fritz Rienecker[7] explains: The translation from the original text does not say "all is new", but „new has become".

On one hand, a complete restoration and healing of the previous life does normally not occur when a decision for Jesus is made. There are always exceptions, of course, as the example of Zacchaeus show - he made amends on a large scale[8].

A great number of circumstances, living conditions and especially the past back until the earliest childhood and even pregnancy are not made new. We are hurt when our basic needs as babies, children and teenagers are not met, when love, appreciation, belonging and comforting are withdrawn from us, or when an early-child relationship to one person was not possible. We are hurt by a lack of care, affection, attention and recognition, and by rejecting, depreciating statements, by comparisons and by abuse of any kind. We are most hurt by the people we love most: by parents, siblings, friends, our partner, teachers or other important authority persons.

Determinations suffice to affect us sustainably. "You are like your father" is what my mother used to say in a deprecatory tone when something in my behaviour reminded her of her divorced husband. This hurt me every single time because indeed, I am the son of my father and I therefore

---

[7] Fritz Rienecker, Sprachlicher Schlüssel zum NT (Language key to the NT), Brunnen Verlag Gießen, page 411
[8] Luke 19:8

have some of his character traits. I finally found the right reply: "You have chosen him, not I." Unfortunately, we are often not aware how these emotional and psychological damages affect our lives today. These experiences are sometimes buried deep down within us, so they are no longer accessible for our mind and our emotions. Ignoring and suppressing them is not a long-term solution because physical and psychological illnesses often force us to deal with past occurrences.

These injuries will not disappear after a decision for Jesus Christ. There are astonishing descriptions about miracles that happen when somebody gives their life to Jesus: somebody was promptly freed from his drug addiction, or healed psychologically and physically, or a depression disappeared, etc. But we have never heard of anyone who was suddenly cured from all negative incidents in their life and who was promptly empowered to do all positive things. If people are not aware of that, then spiritual growth is difficult or even impossible. Confession and pronounced forgiveness or otherwise granted forgiveness are almost unknown tools in Christian counselling today. We have therefore decided to include a chapter about forgiveness. The reference to "hearing" is only indirect, but the answer to "why forgive" still remains unknown to many people.

Some people tend to pretend spiritual growth, or they view their life with Jesus as a spiritual exercise. Others view their decision for Jesus as a kind of life insurance that cannot do any harm. Or people feel that nothing in their lives has changed for the better and then are deeply disappointed, frustrated and turn away from Jesus.

- So-called "backpacker Christians". They know exactly what happened in the past and they keep on carrying their backpack filled with serious incidents throughout all their lives: false determinations by their parents, rejection, or spiritual, emotional and physical abuse of every kind. But they do not know where to put it. Even if they can forgive their tormentors - the fact of their lost childhood or their forced choice of profession remains. The following illustration shall describe these circumstances:
I am walking along the path of my life with a heavy backpack. A bus stops at my side (= Jesus) and offers to take me on with all I am and all I have. I happily accept the offer. But the question is will I enter the bus with my backpack or let Jesus take my backpack off me? If I continue carrying it, then I keep on carrying my burden in the bus (!) and I might even hurt others with protruding objects such as sticks, bottles, umbrellas, etc. Or could I take something out at each stop? Remaining in this illustration: Many bus passengers do not even know they are carrying their burden-backpack, or they view that as normal. They think: "Isn't it great

that the bus carries everything?", but in fact they still carry the heavy backpack themselves.

In other cases, shame prevents that these injuries can come into light. People often think that what happened to them never happened to anyone else, and that the incident must remain concealed. But the story of the fall of man in the Garden of Eden shows: God did not initiate the separation from Adam and Eve. Both hid because they felt ashamed.

There is a good illustration why ignoring and suppressing does not work on the long term. Imagine you are sitting in a boat on a lake. Your injuries and the shame about them are like a beach ball. You press the ball under water with all your power so nobody can see it. (One way to cover your injuries and your shame is by doing so-called good deeds.) But sometimes, in a moment of negligence or weakness, the ball slips out, and you immediately press it under water again. But at some point, your arm will weaken and you will no longer be able to keep the whole ball in hiding. When people grow old and their emotional and physical power weaken, we can often observe changes in them that are quite unsettling. There is an English proverb that gets to the point: "Getting older means getting better or getting bitter."

- Blocked Christians: They do not know where the problem is. But it is a fact that they do not experience growth, they are somehow stuck. Neither as children nor as teenagers and not even as young adults, are we able to deal with the insults and hurt we experienced from our closest friends – we usually push these experiences aside. Therefore, they block us and catch up with us as long as it takes us to face them. Mostly, we only face them when our body has already reacted with diseases and when we have to deal with the "why".

Psychology or psychoanalysis can help finding the causes. This is often a very long (and expensive) process. Psychology or psychoanalysis can reveal, but they cannot eliminate or even heal.
A biblical example is the story of the rich young man. "Teacher, what good thing must I do to get eternal life?" he asked. Jesus answered: "Keep the commandments, love God and love your neighbour as yourself." "All these I have kept," the man answered. What Jesus replied has the following sense: "Then I can tell your weak spot. Your trust is based on your possessions, not on your relationship with me." – But the young man did not want to acknowledge that.

Sometimes, these blocked people are intentionally kept ignorant or encouraged in their wrong attitude with statements such as "In today's world, there is no visible intervention of God. You must bear this, it is your burden." But Jesus says that his yoke is easy and his burden is light[9].

---

[9] Matthew 11:30

- Increase of addictions
  A very interesting article[10] by Shari Langemak explains how addictions develop. Only recently, researchers of Harvard University in Cambridge, USA, have found out that Facebook has similar effects as chocolate, sex and alcohol have. All of these do not only make us happy, but we absolutely want to have them again. The cause is a complex neural network in the brain that is vital for humans and animals.

  Basically, three brain functions are linked in this "reward system": sensory perception, emotion and memory. This makes them the workshop of our learning mechanisms. What is fun will be stored. Addiction expert Mr Falk Kiefer, medical Vice-Director at the Central Institute for Emotional Health in Mannheim, Germany, explains: "We live in a world that is poor in rewards. Among millions of sensory perceptions that reach our brain every minute, we do not only need to recognize those that point to possible dangers, but also those that point to possible rewards."

  Our nervous system filters unconsciously, but at all times. Therefore, we quickly manage to find the next fast-food shop or our children in the milling mass of an amusement park. Instead of processing every sensory perception individually, our brain scans the perceptions for familiar character-

---

[10] German newspaper "DIE WELT" of 14.5.2012 Was Facebook und Sex gemeinsam haben (What Facebook and sex have in common).

istics. For example, it might scan for "little brown-haired girl with glasses". As soon as we find her our neural network gets started. Our body's own happiness hormones, the endorphins, are set free. Similar to the addictive drug opium, they have pain-relieving effects and make us happy. The brain delivers intoxication for our own body if we do something useful. Eating, sex and social contacts are rewarded in every human and in many animal systems. They contribute to survival and to maintenance of the species.

The reward system in our brain marks this positive emotion so that it does not just disappear. The messenger substance dopamine marks this emotion and thus contributes to the reward-based learning processes. "Dopamine is set free with every positive experience. Thus, not only the stimulus, but also the situation is marked", explains Kiefer.

But this originally vital mechanism can turn to be dangerous. Addictions have their origins in these reward systems, especially the addiction to alcohol. Addicts are running the gauntlet on a daily basis: ads, bars, supermarkets and even old friends – almost the entire environment is a signal in the reward system for alcohol. And it remains there for a lifetime. "The reward memory cannot be deleted", warns Kiefer. This is why these patients are always in danger of falling back into their addictions, even after many years of abstinence."

The statement in the last two sentences – that, by the way, we do not agree to – leads us to our next observation:

- We tend to take facts for the truth. We would like to explain that as follows:
A good example is the story of Sara and Abraham[11]. Fact was that Sara was 90 years old and far beyond her menopause. But the truth was: She conceived Isaac because God wanted her to.
Another example is the story of the daughter of Jairus[12]. Jesus was held back by healing the woman who had been subject to bleeding for twelve years, and in the meantime the girl had died. In Mark 5:35 the bystanders say: "Your daughter is dead, why bother the teacher anymore?" But Jesus answered: "Don't be afraid; just believe!"
And there is the amusing story in Acts 19:35-36: The city clerk of Ephesus claimed that the image of Artemis had fallen from heaven and that this fact was undeniable.
The story of Lazarus[13] illustrates very well where we can get stuck. Jesus learns of Lazarus' illness but remains two more days where he was and only then walks into Judea. He already knew that Lazarus had died (verse 14). Martha says on his arrival: "Lord, if you had been here, my brother would not have died." Mary says the same in

---

[11] Genesis 18
[12] Mark 5:22-43
[13] John 11

verse 32. And then Jesus asks: "Where have you laid him?", and he weeps. Before he can perform the miracle, the bystanders must remove the stone (verse 39). The stone stands for what is in the way from the human side. Without the removal of the stone, there is no miracle. Martha still doubts, but the bystanders finally remove the stone. And Lazarus comes out! When the Holy Spirit shows us facts that we should ignore, we should do so, with trembling hearts.

This means that facts are no obstacles for the Holy Spirit, neither in our lives nor in the lives of others. These facts are valid in the visible world, but not in the invisible world. Fact was that Lazarus had died, but truth was that Jesus raised him from the dead.

- A last observation is the understanding of the tasks of priests and prophets. In the Old Testament, the priest brought people before God. The supreme example is Moses who interceded for the people of Israel before God. We can say that he acted as an intermediary. Jesus is the high priest in the order of Melchizedek[14] and reconciled us with God the Father. Hence, a priest brings people to God.

  A prophet does the opposite: He brings God to the people. Examples are Daniel[15], who received directions in the form of impressions and dreams.

---

[14] Hebrews 7
[15] Daniel 3:31-4:34

Joshua received all kinds of instructions on how to conquer the cities of the Promised Land. And Hezekiah received during his severe illness a direct promise by a prophet that God would prolong his life by 15 years[16].

In the New Testament, the Holy Spirit assumes this task. Jesus promises that in his farewell address: "He will not speak on his own; he will speak only what he hears[17]."

So what could counselling be like when integrating these observations? Counselling with as few harmful side effects or none at all? Maybe you have been ill recently, and you had to take medication. When we read the patient information leaflet (that often is as large as a newspaper) we wonder how many negative side effects can occur. But when God acts, there are no harmful side effects. That is what we are looking for, and that is what we would like to outline in the following chapters.

How did we personally encounter this kind of counselling?

In the mid-1980ies we oriented ourselves anew to the Holy Spirit and we asked and expected him to intervene more. In October 1987, we had met for prayer with our friend Wolfgang Bienert. The reason was the severe illness of Beate, the wife of a good

---

[16] 2 Kings 20:6

[17] John 16:13b. For Jesus there are similar verses: Matthew 10:27; John 8:26b

friend. She had suffered a brain haemorrhage the day before and had lapsed into a coma. We started to pray for healing, but we somehow sensed that this was not the intention of the Spirit of Jesus. He then took over and showed us in an impression how Jesus stood at the foot end of Beate's bed and offered her a decision to give her life to him. We addressed the spirit of Beate in prayer and encouraged her to make a decision for Jesus. We later had the impression that she had done so. Wolfgang later received a bible passage that confirmed that impression. Beate died two days later.

With this incident our "training period" in Hearing Prayer, Hearing Blessings and Hearing Counselling started.

This form of counselling may also be called prophetic counselling because God himself acts and intervenes in the life of a man or a woman. However, we prefer to speak of Hearing Counselling because we are fully dependent upon God. Hearing God is not a talent, it is a gift. When he does not speak or give pictured impressions, we cannot and shall not pass anything on – especially not any well-intentioned advice.

About Hearing

At first, we would like to make some observations about hearing.

The sense of hearing is the first sense that an embryo develops, namely already 14 weeks after conception. And hearing is the last sense that vanishes when a person dies (and when his/her hearing is intact). Thus, hearing plays an essential role in our lives. Just like we have physical senses, we also have spiritual senses. They have been revitalized when we made our decision for Jesus and when the Spirit of Jesus correlated with our sleeping or dead spirit[18]. In order to hear God's voice we need our inner ear, our "ear of the heart". But how can we hear God?

Hearing Prayer starts with us which means, every day we should enter God's Presence in quietness and speak out what is inside of us – in our soul and our spirit. We can learn to tell everything to our Father. When we talk to him, we will also hear what he says. We can talk with him about everything, like a child, without being ashamed.

---

[18] John 3:3-8

These four keys are helpful in hearing God:

1. A quiet spot, a quiet atmosphere.
   God does not want to drown out the world, even though he could easily do that. He does not want to enforce our attention but he waits until we turn to him - and to our neighbour who needs help.

2. God's voice in our hearts is like many spontaneous thoughts.
   The Holy Spirit speaks to most people in the form of spontaneous thoughts, images, feelings or impressions. Have you ever experienced that, while sitting in a car, you suddenly had the idea to pray for someone? We think this is the voice of God that calls us to prayer. The question is now: How did God's voice sound? Was it an audible voice or a spontaneous thought? Most people would say that God's voice came spontaneously.

3. Our thoughts become quiet.
   We ask the Holy Spirit to steady everything in us. We consciously place our thoughts under the protection of the blood of Jesus.

4. Focus our attention.
   We redirect our attention away from our problems and other people and focus on the Father, on Jesus and on the Holy Spirit.

Besides our inner ears we have inner eyes, or "eyes of the heart". When we tell someone "Imagine how an elephant looks like!", then most people can imagine an elephant with their inner eyes, even though he is not really there. We place these inner eyes and ears at God's disposal and ask the Holy Spirit to open them for what he has seen and heard in God's throne room. Just like Jesus saw what the Father wants to do (John 5:19).

We have also experienced that we can smell something with an inner sense of smell. Heinrich sometimes smells burnt flesh when an evil spirit has left a body. And Hildegard has sensed a godly fragrance that no perfume could ever spread.

In summary: All our senses are in contact with the Holy Spirit, so that he can tell us what he wants to tell and that he can trigger emotions or images that he wants to share with us.

Why does the Holy Spirit want to talk directly?

The Holy Spirit wants to help us on our way with Jesus to go to the Father. He sees our struggles to follow Jesus, to serve and to make everything as good as possible in our family, our neighbourhood, our job and our church. And he knows that we can never do that by ourselves, not from our own power and even not out of love. The Holy Spirit wants to help us – not because we have earned his help, but because we need it. We need it so much.

This is an important further development compared to the Old Testament. Ecclesiastes 3:11 says: "...no one can fathom what God has done from beginning to end." But when Jesus went back to heaven, he sent us the Holy Spirit. The Holy Spirit explains to us what God the Father would like to do. And Ecclesiastes is right when saying: We cannot find this out by our own efforts.

This experience is nothing new. Hildegard von Bingen, a woman who lived in the 11th century in Germany, experienced that[19]:

"And my soul climbs – as God wills – in this vision up into the heights of the firmament. But I do not see these things with the outer eyes and I do not hear

---

[19] Wibke Becker, Frankfurter Allgemeine Sonntagszeitung of 13.05.2012: Meine Seele steigt in der Schau empor (translated).

them with the outer ears, neither do I perceive them with the thoughts of my heart nor with any involvement of my five senses. I rather see them only in my soul, with my physical eyes open, so I shall never experience the unconsciousness of an ecstasy. But I see it being awake, day and night. I keep all that I see and learn in these visions in my memory for a long time, because as soon as I see or hear them, they enter my memory. I see and I hear and I know at the same time, and I immediately learn what I know. But what I do not see, I do not know ..."

Based on this hearing, seeing and sentient attitude we now would like to describe the impacts that we can experience during Hearing Prayer, Hearing Blessings and Hearing Counselling.

One observation beforehand: What is invisible to us was created before the visible, and the visible was created out of the invisible[20]. God was before the earth, and he will continue to be after the earth will have vanished.[21]
We are children of the Enlightenment who declare something as non-existent when we cannot see it. But listening to the Holy Spirit enables us to assume a godly perspective that reaches far beyond the limited human possibilities of the visible world. We have always experienced God's perspective to be larger, wider, deeper, and to be healing.

---

[20] Genesis 1:1 et seqq.
[21] Isaiah 65:17

Hearing Prayer

There is a very good theological introduction about Hearing Prayer in the first part of the book by Ursula and Manfred Schmidt[22]. Here, we would like to focus on the practical aspects of hearing.

Hearing Prayer

Here is a quotation by Søren Kierkegaard:
I first thought praying is talking. But I learned that praying is not just becoming silent, but it is hearing. This is it: To pray does not mean to listen to oneself speaking. Prayer involves becoming silent, and being silent, and waiting until God is heard.

Hearing Prayer means turning to the Holy Spirit and listening to what he wants to say. A matching bible passage is Ephesians 6:18: "And pray in the Spirit on all occasions with all kinds of prayers and requests." This already happened in the Old Testament times when Daniel prayed and the Archangel Gabriel came to him[23].

Jesus promised us that the Holy Spirit will come and teach us (see the Gospel of John[24]). According to our experience, the Holy Spirit often talks via images or pictured impressions. Why? With images, the Holy Spirit can circumvent, and even avoid, our minds. There is a saying: "A picture is worth a thousand

---

[22] Ursula und Manfred Schmidt, Hörendes Gebet (Hearing Prayer), GGE Geistliche Gemeinde-Erneuerung (2009)
[23] Daniel 9:23
[24] John 14:26 and John 16:12-15

words." A picture can describe a situation so precisely that we can only stand in awe. Jesus has often spoken in images and parables. Moreover, we can "enter" into a picture and the Holy Spirit can show us more details. Sometimes, it is a whole line of pictures, almost a short movie. The hearing person should not interrupt too soon, but shall look about, ask whether there is more to see in that picture, see what becomes of it and remain contemplative because the picture sometimes changes. By the way, after some time we can enter the same picture again and ask the Holy Spirit to reveal more details.

The Holy Spirit can also communicate with bible passages. It is especially interesting when we only receive a verse and a number, e.g., "Psalm 3, verse 4" and we do not know what stands there. The Holy Spirit can also communicate to us via a direct word of Jesus, via an emotion, a feeling, or even physical pain. Once, Hildegard suddenly had stomach pains when praying and hearing and she told us. The woman for whom we prayed immediately said: "That is so obvious to me; I have always swallowed too much all my life."

When hearing, we do not want to set any limits for the Holy Spirit, how he wants to act and intervene. At times, Heinrich starts to cry and he does not know why. Sometimes out of joy because the Holy Spirit is about to say something personal, sometimes because he sees the tears in God's eyes when the Father looks at his beloved child that has finally come to him. Every now and then, the Holy Spirit speaks directly to

the seeking person. Therefore, we first ask: "Did you have an impression? Please dare to tell us."
Then, we talk with the seeking person about what we have heard or seen. From time to time, there is a direct answer to a question, and very often the images and impressions of the praying persons match with each other or complement each other.
Every now and then, the images are without any evident correlation to the desire or the problem of the seeking person. But we often experience that they address the real cause or problem of the seeking person, although this is not obvious to them.
We always speak to the seeking person with all due respect about what we have received: When we have received a picture, a bible passage, a direct word, a feeling in our body, a song text … we say:
I have the impression that …
I have the feeling that …
We do not say: God has shown me that you are/must do …

Of course, there is a certain risk that these pictures and impressions do not come from God. Therefore, it is essential to turn to the Holy Spirit at the beginning of each prayer, to focus on him only. It is important to have respect for the seeking person and to ask him/her to check and test everything and to hold on to what is good. We humans can err. It is good to practice hearing prayer with three people, because reciprocal corrections are important.

Before we speak out loud what we heard, we shall check if it is according to Jesus' will:
- It should be positive, encouraging, also advising.
- It should correspond to what the bible says.

Then we ask the seeking person what he/she feels or thinks what the Holy Spirit has shared. Very often, the individual impressions of the praying persons are like different puzzle pieces that form a whole. That is wonderful and cannot be made up by humans.

If we have the impression that we should touch the seeking person (e.g., to take them in our arms) we should ask him/her beforehand if this is alright. Physical touch can trigger or release a lot, if encouraged by the Holy Spirit. In today's world, physical touch without hidden motives has become quite seldom. Sometimes, men or women just want to be hugged in order to feel that somebody passes on God's love.

Nowadays, physical touch can be perceived quite ambiguously, because sexuality is ever-present. Therefore, a downright industry for physical touch has developed, as an article in a German newspaper describes[25]: Wellness treatments in a day spa or cuddling courses are offered. Does a managing director ever receive real hugs?

---

[25] „Anfassen, Berühren, Streicheln" (Touching, Caressing) by Thomas Haberl, Süddeutsche Zeitung Magazin of 17.10.2008

The reason for a defective relationship to physical touch is that modern man has a disordered relationship to proximity. Couple therapist, Mr Wolfgang Schmidbauer, observes in the above-mentioned article: "We have become more anxious. Relationships are increasingly characterized by retreat, avoidance and blockades. Many people are so unsettled and so easily offended that they prefer to shift intimacy into a professional area where they can control it."

When touching people, it is important that we do not only radiate human warmth, but that we do what the Holy Spirit tells us to do. Maybe it is about loving the seeking person like we would love a child, by telling them what the heavenly Father wants to tell. Maybe they just want to cry about what has been done to them. Some people want to be hugged (!) and at the same time they want to express their anger. And still they want to experience a blessing later on, receive a blessing hand or a hug before they leave (signalling that everything is fine in God's eyes).

Furthermore, it is important that the seeking person does not focus on the praying people, but on what Jesus and the Father have for him/her. The praying people are only human beings who might disappoint them at some stage.

But the seeking persons always need to check what they have heard. They can accept it or re-think about it or ask Jesus about it. They can reject what they have heard, like in the parable of the rich young man[26]. Those who practice hearing prayer are not responsible that the seeking persons implement what they have received. Advice or help can be given, but no control. This is a matter of the Holy Spirit to talk to that person.

Preparation

The team
It is advisable that there are 2 – 3 people in a prayer team. If there are more, then the prayer session might last very long. And one single praying person might find it difficult to pray and hear without the correction or confirmation of another person. Furthermore, it is helpful to have a woman and a man in one team. They perceive the world differently and they think differently. This is how God has preconceived the world: Adam could only cope with the world together with Eve, and vice versa. It is gets difficult when Eve decides by herself, as she did in the parable of the forbidden fruit.

It is good to practice hearing the Father. We have observed that it is a lot easier to hear for other people than hearing for oneself. Probably we are often part of the problem and cannot hear for ourselves with an open mind. In 1 Peter 3:9 it says: "… repay evil with blessing, because to this you were called so that you may inherit a blessing." God's indirect way

---

[26] Matthew 19:16

of blessing, namely by the detour via other people, is one of the secrets of God.

It is a great help to start as a "Hearing Prayer trainee" with one or two experienced people. We have often experienced that the "trainee" soon receives his/her first impressions for others. A very important bible passage says: "What we are is plain to God, and I hope it is also plain to your conscience."[27] The Father looks affectionately at his children and he shares with us what is in his heart.

Putting our vast experience on hold
Sometimes, what we have experienced and seen before when praying for others stands in the way. It is not about praying with talented people, but it is about a divine encounter with God the Father, Jesus and the Holy Spirit.

And that is absolutely different. People are often a hindrance. God's talking surpasses by far anything that we could ever collect from experiences or wisdom, or what people have researched in all kinds of sciences.

When praying and hearing, it is ALWAYS about a one-of-a-kind individual and about the individual life of that person under consideration of their current situation, their childhood, their denomination, their job situation, and much more. No psychologist can analyse the complexity of an individual, like Hilarion

---

[27] 2 Corinthians 5:11

Petzold once said in an interview.[28] Psychologists fail because of the complexity of the individual: "We always deal with a human being as a whole; we need to consider the whole story of their life, their current situation and their life plans, as well as the many different schools and models of psychotherapy."

But this is no problem for the Holy Spirit. He ALWAYS has something unique for every single child of the Father, something out of his love. His talking is not something human that is passed through us, and it is not a well-meant advice from a book. His words come from the love of the Father. The Holy Spirit searches all things, even the deep things of God[29] and those of the human being. The Holy Spirit can truly help. And he knows everything.

IT IS ABOUT LIFE. All people are born as originals, and many die as a copy because Satan, the hinderer and confounder, does not want the original person to evolve. We have NEVER received the same impression for two people, not even close.

We can do nothing by ourselves
We confess in front of the visible and the invisible world that we do not know anything, but that we want to focus entirely on the Holy Spirit so that he

---

[28] Prof Hilaron Petzold: Die Psychotherapie der Zukunft (Psychotherapy today); magazine „Psychologie heute", June 2012
[29] 1 Corinthians 2:10

will fill our thinking, our feeling and our doing. He takes the load off us: We do not have to produce anything. The Holy Spirit knows that we rely on him. He has never abandoned or betrayed us. But we sometimes had to wait. There must not be any pressure that something needs to happen. But we can ask the Holy Spirit to talk and to act. If we do not receive any impressions, we can ask the Holy Spirit what blocks us. And he will help us.

What Hearing Prayer is NOT
- Unchecked interceding for the wishes of the seeking person.
- Telling the seeking person my good wishes.
- Interceding out of my vast intercession experience. Intercession is important and has its role and its value in prayer life. But in the case of hearing prayer, we do not act as priests, but prophetically. It is about learning what God has in his heart and not about what we think he shall or could do.
- Applying my human advice and knowledge of human nature.
- Implementing scientific knowledge and findings.

Bible passages about hearing what the Father wants or says

John 5:19 et seqq.
"Very truly I tell you, the Son can do nothing by himself; he can do only what he sees his Father doing, because whatever the Father does the Son also does.

For the Father loves the Son and shows him all he does. Yes, and he will show him **even greater** works than these, so that you will be amazed."

John 6:45
"It is written in the Prophets (Isaiah 54:13): 'They will all be taught by God.' Everyone who has heard the Father and learned from him comes to me."

John 4:34
"My food," said Jesus "is to do the will of him who sent me and to finish his work."

John 6:63
"The Spirit gives life; the flesh counts for nothing. The words I have spoken to you—they are full of the Spirit and life."

Exodus 33:13
"If you are pleased with me, teach me your ways so I may know you and continue to find favour with you."

1 Corinthians 14:23-25
Hearing (prophetic) prayer as a possibility for mission.

Ephesians 2:8 et seqq.
8 For it is by grace you have been saved, through faith—and this is not from yourselves, it is the gift of God (saved life and hearing prayer) —
9 not by works, so that no one can boast.

10 For we are God's handiwork, created in Christ Jesus to do good works, which God **prepared in advance for us to do**."

There are three prerequisites to practice Hearing Prayer:

The main prerequisite is to have made a personal decision for Jesus Christ and to live it. Closely connected with that is to have received the Holy Spirit.
The second prerequisite is the willingness and the ability for Hearing Prayer – i.e., not to pray out of our own hearts and out of our compassion for others. That means that I acknowledge that there comes nothing good and helpful out of myself.
The third prerequisite is to make oneself fully dependant on the speaking and acting of the Holy Spirit.

What is so extraordinary about it?
In one sentence: When we have time, the Holy Spirit, the Father and Jesus always have time, too. This is the most incredible thing I have ever heard. God, the Father of Jesus, the creator of heaven and earth and the universe, who has been reigning forever, always has time for every single one of his children.

When I take time, the Father always has time, too. One bible passage that states that truth, as Moses experienced, is written in Exodus 33:9: God comes down in the pillar of cloud **at the moment when** Moses enters the tent.

Hearing Blessing

Hearing Blessing is based on Hearing Prayer. Hearing Blessing is, so to speak, a continuation of Hearing Prayer. We do not talk about "asking for a blessing", but we talk about "granting someone a blessing, pronouncing a blessing over someone, putting the blessing on someone". That means that I act in the name of Jesus and the Holy Spirit and I lay the blessing that I heard onto the seeking person.

Of course, it is essential that I have heard something from the Holy Spirit before. Or the Holy Spirit helps me by giving me an image or an impression or a bible passage, and he helps me to interpret so that a word of blessing is in there for the seeking person.

The objective of Hearing Blessing is that the person seeking a blessing receives an experience, a divine encounter with the living God.

Nothing more and nothing less.

- He/she shall experience that God the Father, Jesus and the Holy Spirit love him/her, despite of all imperfections.
- Despite of all circumstances in which he/she lives.
- Despite all experiences he/she has made so far.
- Regardless of how long he/she has lived with Christ.

- He/she shall experience that the Father knows him/her. Can you guess what that means? God knows this individual person by his/her name, out of almost 7 billion people. Most people are afraid of being neither known nor loved. Just look at the different TV programs with all these people who would do anything to be known and loved: talk shows, talent shows, jungle camps, etc. The biggest desire of every human being is to be known by the Father and to be loved by him. This is his/her destination since the beginning of time.
- The Father loves him/her NOW. And has always loved him/her. And will always love him/her.
- Even though he/she has failed.
- Regardless about how much he/she has achieved.
- Despite of his/her efforts.
- Because he/she is his child.
- And because God the Father cannot bear to be without him/her.

The objective of Hearing Blessing is NOT:

- Speaking out of my vast experience into the life of the seeking person.
- Giving good advice.
- Unchecked interceding for the wishes of the seeking person and blessing them for that (I underline: unchecked. We will later come back on how to check that).
- Pouring out my bible or book knowledge over the seeking person.

- Smoothing over the fears and insecurity of the seeking person. Many of those who come are afraid of God: What will happen? What if God says something devastating?
- Pretending what the seeking person told "is not so bad, we can manage that …"

Example:
The Holy Spirit has given an image to the praying team where a child is sitting on the lap of the Father. Then, led by the Holy Spirit, we might lay the following blessing on the seeking person:
"I bless you with the status of childhood that you have with Abba, your Heavenly Father. I bless you with all rights that a child has in the house of its Father, e.g., unhindered access to the Father's throne room. The Father has time for you, he is willing to protect his child, and he laughs and cries with it …"

The Holy Spirit will add more and new thoughts, so that the seeking person notices: It is not the praying team that is talking from their experience, but it is the Holy Spirit who is talking through the blessing person.

We would like to underline again that the praying team shall not ask for a blessing, but that they specifically declare the blessing over the seeking person. This is emphasised in the Aaronic blessing[30]: "So they (the blessing persons) will **put** my name on the Israel-

---

[30] Book of Numbers 6:22-26

ites, and I will bless them" (Book of Numbers 6:27). The same in Book of Deuteronomy 10:8 "Pronounce blessings in his name."

Attributing a blessing

These are examples for attributing a blessing to someone in the context of hearing blessings:
"I bless you with godly wisdom for this situation in your family/job."
"We bless you with fatherhood/motherhood for your children."
"I bless you with the power of Jesus, so you can and will forgive."

Hearing Blessing is clearly based on Hearing Prayer, because if I did not hear anything I cannot pronounce a blessing.

The Holy Spirit showed us that we call the gifts into life that the Father has placed in every single person. Sometimes, the Holy Spirit will show these talents or gifts, but sometimes they remain concealed.

Corresponding Bible Passages

Genesis 27
- Blessings have effect, even when attributed to the wrong person – this is shown in the story of Jacob, who has gained by trickery the father's blessing[31].
- A blessing cannot be withdrawn[32]! That is an astonishing fact.
- There is a special blessing of a father for his children at the end of his life.

Balaam
The story of Balaam is a prime example for Hearing Blessing[33]. Balaam cannot follow Balak's instruction, but he **must** do what God says. (Unfortunately, Balaam later seduced the people of Israel to worship foreign Gods.)

Psalm 118:26
"From the house of the Lord we bless you."

Even Jesus is blessed by a man and by a woman (!)[34]
Old Simeon blessed Jesus – the Holy Spirit had told him that he would see the Messiah and had led him to go into the temple. Then, the prophetess Anna came and blessed Jesus as well.

---

[31] Genesis 27:27-29
[32] Genesis 27:33-40
[33] Book of Numbers, chapters 22-24
[34] Luke 2:25 -38

When Jesus sends out his disciples to preach[35] he promises them that the Holy Spirit will come to their help; especially when they need to speak in front of potentates and governors or when they need to defend themselves.

---

[35] Matthew 10, especially verse 20

Hearing Counselling

Hearing Counselling goes beyond Hearing Blessing and mostly needs more time than a short blessing session on a Sunday after a church service. It often makes more sense to set up an appointment for a counselling session or a spiritual counselling hour.

One remark about the word "counselling": It is not only about a person's soul, but it concerns the whole person. In the old days, people said: "A village has 60 souls", and that meant, of course, living people. Counselling is about the person as a whole, not only about a part of them. The word "counselling" does not merely mean to give good counsel, but to counsel the person with what God has for them.

In contrast to Hearing Prayer and Hearing Blessing, we ask the Holy Spirit what he would like to address next. We can hereby refer to James[36] who writes: "If any of you lacks wisdom, you should ask God, who gives generously to all without finding fault, and it will be given to you."
Furthermore, Hearing Counselling is what many people are really looking for. It is possible, in small steps, to do it in an after-service session on a Sunday (following the motto: "If people don't come and ask for counselling, then the counselling will come to them"). One reason why people do not ask for counselling is that they have a wrong idea about counselling. They

---

[36] James 1:5

suppose that they have to embarrassingly confess all their sins in front of another person who will shake the head with a wagging finger and who will impose a punishment and insist they shall never sin again, try to do it better next time, improve their efforts, read the bible more, more of this and more of that... In fact, when the method described here is used, only the symptoms will be treated, but not their cause. Nothing fundamental in the life of the seeking person will change.

If we look at the parable of the prodigal son[37] we notice that the father is not interested at all in his son's sins. On the contrary, he is delighted upon his son's return and starts with the restoration of the son into his original status[38].

Admittedly, displeasing things can emerge during Hearing Counselling if the Holy Spirit wants to address them. But the seeking person always has the freedom to end the counselling session at any given time. The aim of the Holy Spirit is that everything exposed by the light becomes visible – and everything that is illuminated becomes a light[39]. What had been a burden will be changed into freedom for the children of God, and it will become a help for the seeking person and for others.

---

[37] Luke 15:11-32
[38] Luke 15:21-22
[39] Ephesians 5:13-14

One example of application in Hearing Counselling is how to deal with demoralizing statements by other people, such as "You are worthless. You will never be successful. You are like your father. Other people do it better". Generally, it is not enough to pray that these painful thoughts disappear. They will come back like a boomerang at the next opportunity. It is necessary to ask the Holy Spirit what the origins or causes are. When the Holy Spirit reveals the cause, i.e., the root of the problem, he will also show what shall be done next. Sometimes, people who were close to the seeking person in their childhood or adolescence have become guilty. According to our experiences, it is helpful that the counsellors[40] express a representative confession of guilt in front of the seeking person; this often has healing effects.

It is also essential that the seeking person declares that they will separate from these burdening thoughts. We can then, in the name of Jesus, erase the accusing thoughts[41] like the sun sweeps away the morning mist. Then, we ask the Holy Spirit to fill the room that has been set free and that used to be occupied by the accusing thoughts. No empty room must remain: The room that the thoughts had occupied must be filled with the presence of the Holy Spirit. Jesus himself has called our attention to that[42].

---

[40] See PRACTICAL TIPS AND TOOLS – Bible passages for the representative confession of guilt.
[41] Isaiah 44:22
[42] Luke 11:24-26

The next step is to bless the seeking person with power in order to reject new negative thoughts that will attack him/her in the near future: "I **do not want** this anymore."

It is highly encouraging for the receiving and for the blessing person to experience how the Holy Spirit gives directions, reveals connections, brings the truth to light and exposes secrets.

There are countless people in our church services who carry burdens they do not even know about. The iceberg example is helpful to explain the situation: The iceberg (person) does **not** move in the direction of the wind (comparable to the person's will), but moves in the direction of the current (the subconscious mind). Only the Holy Spirit can help and show what was pushed away into sub consciousness. These causes can be manifold: negative thoughts and determinations, abuse, suicidal intentions, attempted abortion by the mother and other traumatic experiences that are locked away and that are, metaphorically speaking, fermenting under a concrete lid. They prevent us from becoming what the Father has laid within us before the creation of the world[43]. Curses have destructive impacts[44] and must be lifted.

---

[43] Ephesians 1:4
[44] Zechariah 5:4

What to do, practically speaking?

In case of an existing burden or strain we ask the Holy Spirit to reveal the cause or to show a starting point at which HE wants to approach it. In case of unclear symptoms we ask the Holy Spirit to give us clarity and wisdom.

Especially in the case of older people the so-called symptom of the "concrete lid" often appears. The concrete lid stands for one or several experiences that date back a long time, but that have never been addressed or treated. Instead, they were ignored and pushed away with all might. It is, metaphorically speaking, as if all traumatic experiences were dumped into a den that was then closed off with a concrete lid so that these negative experiences would never come up and interfere with present life. This works as long as the human power is strong enough (cf. the example of the ball under water in the Introduction chapter, backpacker Christians, page 15/16). If the power ceases, as it often does with age or illness, then the concrete lid will lift itself and the past experiences that had been locked up for years break out.

One possibility to deal with that is to look at the main problem together with the Holy Spirit and to ask HIM to reveal the part that shall be revealed and that shall come into light. It is necessary that the seeking person has great trust in the counsellors and is prepared to address their problem. The counsellors must act very gently and carefully in order to do only what the Holy Spirit wants to do, and not more. Many burdened people perceive the disclosure of their traumatic experiences as a threat to their lives. Suppressing the problems has enabled them to survive in the past, but now it has become a threat. What previously helped to survive is now a burden. A lot of time and patience is often required until the affected persons are ready to let the concrete lid go and to face their past.

It is often not helpful to make a harsh diagnosis. Instead it is better if the Holy Spirit talks gently to the seeking person. The seeking person must be encouraged, the Father's love for them and their child ship with the Father must be confirmed– despite of everything that happened. Sometimes, the Holy Spirit reminds us to place everybody (the seeking person, their family, the praying team) again under the protection of the blood of Jesus Christ.[45]

When the situation has become clear we ask the Holy Spirit to show us what to do next. Sometimes, it is helpful to be experienced, but sometimes it is NOT. Why? Because the Holy Spirit acts with every person individually; and therefore our connection with him is the only key – it is not our experience. He knows what to do next – he knows it better and more precisely and more gently.

---

[45] PRACTICAL TIPS AND TOOLS: The blood of Jesus protects

There is a very helpful example of a pastor in the U.S. who was praying with a woman. He asked her what she had seen or received. "Nothing", she said. "Really nothing?", he replied. "No, nothing", she said. "Really nothing at all?", he replied again. "Well, to be honest I have seen something red", she said. The pastor replied: "What is the colour red to you, what does red stand for?" "It stands for the blood of Jesus", was the reply. "And what does that stand for?" "For forgiveness", she answered. Then the pastor asked: „Do you have any issues with forgiveness? " "Well, yes, in a very profound and personal matter." They had reached the point that the Holy Spirit wanted them to reach. The colour red led them to forgiveness and to deliverance.

When the Holy Spirit has talked he will also give an interpretation and show the next step.
Which tools or weapons shall be used next?
Sometimes the Holy Spirit acts sovereignly, for example by having the person rest in the Spirit[46].
Or is it enough for today?
It might be advisable that all praying team members will hear and listen closely again.

---

[46] A person is seemingly absent or in a sleep-like state in which the Holy Spirit can operate in a special manner. The person might fall down and lay on the ground, might be seated or standing (in that case, the person often sways). One or all of the praying persons shall remain with the seeking person until he/she wakes up.

If it becomes clear that the seeking person carries guilt with themselves, it is necessary that they confess it and that forgiveness is granted to them. If other people have become guilty towards the seeking person, their forgiveness is the best way to remove the power that this guilt has in their life: forgiveness has healing impacts in the forgiving person.[47]

There is a very convincing bible passage to underline this (Ephesians 5:13-14):
"But everything exposed by the light becomes visible—and everything that is illuminated becomes a light. This is why it is said: 'Wake up, sleeper, rise from the dead, and Christ will shine on you.' "

This means that the wound will become a gift, a talent. Due to his family situation Heinrich had a "father's wound"; this is why he now has a special understanding and love for fatherless people.

Sometimes, the seeking person cannot forgive. The English language has some expressions that show that a person who cannot forgive does harm to themselves (I am annoyed, I bear enmity, I have something on my heart). It is important to know that forgiveness is first of all an act of will; the emotion will come later, slowly. But at times, the wounds are so deep that this act of will is impossible for the seeking person. But Jesus can act anyway, as you will read

---

[47] See chapter about "Forgiveness"

in the example of the "double backpack" in the chapter Incidents).

End of the Hearing Counselling Session

At the end, we bless the seeking person and anoint them if appropriate.[48] It is important for us as counsellors that we do not carry any responsibility. Did you know that the word "responsibility" in the sense of „bearing responsibility" or even "putting someone in charge" does not occur in the bible? When Jesus sent out his disciples, he did NOT burden them with responsibility! We are servants at the hand of the Holy Spirit. This creates freedom. Jesus carries the responsibility.

Of course, this does not mean that we shall trifle with someone or something – this is not possible if we keep close to the Holy Spirit.

Counselling is something that is exciting and encouraging. The seeking person realises that God is not interested in his sins (cf. the father in the parable of the prodigal son), but that he is interested in leading his child into the freedom of the Father's love. And Hearing Counselling is also encouraging to the counsellor because they can experience that the Holy Spirit acts truly individually.

---

[48] PRACTICAL TIPS AND TOOLS: Anointing with oil

We often practice Hearing Prayer, Hearing Blessing and Hearing Counselling in a shortened version at the end of the service in our church and in other churches, at church weekends, seminars and Alpha course weekends.

Eugen Biser, one of the important German catholic theologians of our times, writes: „**The Gospel is a therapeutic one. Or none at all.**"

Forgiveness

Psychological and medical research have discovered the field of „forgiveness" only in the mid 1990ies, even though it is one of the most important topics that decides about a person's happiness. Our deepest and most passionate emotions are involved, i.e., love and hate. Therefore, the ability and the disability to forgive shape the quality of our relationships. Psychologist Axel Wolf says that renouncing of retaliation, as preached by Jesus Christ, is a decisive but not often practiced step of mankind – much to the damage of men and women. But careful: It is not about justifying injustice! Jesus as well as Stephen prayed: "Father, forgive them, for they do not know what they are doing[49]".

Why is forgiving so difficult?

We could say: "This person is not worth it, I will not deal with him or her. I cancel this relationship and then everything is going to be alright." But no, it will not be alright. Pushing something aside does not help remove the pain and the wounds that somebody else has inflicted upon us.

When we are deeply hurt, our mind will save it as an "unsolved matter", and it will bounce back into our lives. When this unsolved matter meets a current

---

[49] Luke 23:34 and Acts 7:60

conflict, the hurt is as painful as it was 20 years ago, as if it had only been yesterday. Let's assume that someone came and told Hildegard that this book is "mediocre"; then she would remember her German teacher who told her more than 40 years ago that her performance was exactly that: mediocre. The wound of this pain is now healed, but a scar remains. Suffered harm will remain saved in our brains, but it will not hurt any more.

Furthermore, we carry the principle of justice in ourselves and therefore feel the need of satisfying injustice. We request that the offender at least shows repentance and asks for forgiveness. Because this striving for compensation is deeply anchored within us, it is that much more difficult for us, through forgiving, to create an "assumed imbalance" to our disadvantage. This is how we feel. Nathaniel Branden[50] writes: "What is so tragic in many people's lives is that, having the choice to be right or to be happy, they prefer to be right. And this has consequences."

Forgiving is sometimes so difficult that we rather prefer to fall ill than to let our rights go. Comprehensive studies prove the influence of the soul on the development and the course of an illness: Every time we remember, for whatever reason or incident, mortification or a wound, our blood pressure increases. Adrenaline is released into our blood and leads to

---

[50] Nathaniel Branden: Die 6 Säulen des Selbstwertgefühls (The 6 pillars of self-esteem) , Piper edition 2003

high blood pressure, narrowed blood vessels and circulation problems - because a physical or emotional controversy with the offender does not take place.

Scientists who have dealt with psychosomatics have done research about what effects hurtful experiences in the childhood have on the development of pain syndromes. And they discovered a connection: Patients with indistinct pains reported significantly more often about abuse, disputes of the parents or missing love and care. Those who have experienced massive rejection or neglect of their basic needs in their childhood, adolescence or early adulthood later suffer from a weaker immune system. The scientists confirmed that body, soul, spirit and environment are interdependent. Symptoms that our body expresses in consequence of hurting experiences might be: headaches, stomach-aches, dizziness, depression, insomnia, rheumatism, arthritis, fibromyalgia, skin diseases, asthma, cancer, especially breast cancer with women, and men often have back problems.

Many people complain about back problems. But in six of seven cases, doctors cannot find a physical cause of chronic back-aches. Only in one of seven cases the cause of the back problems can be detected, it is often a diminishment of the intervertebral space.

We repeat: People who do not deal with a harmful situation and who do not "let it go" will be less resilient; and those who hold on to their rancour will have a weaker immune system than people who talk about their emotional pains and who can let them go because they have forgiven.

There is a good example that illustrates this issue. In medieval times, many European fortresses and castles featured a "debtor's prison" or "guilt tower": All debtors who could not pay their debts were imprisoned here. The task of the lord was to keep the debtors alive and to guard them until they had paid all their debts. This "debtor's tower" could often be seen from the lord's bedroom, so that the lord could check if the guards had taken their positions.

This is our situation if we do not forgive people who have become guilty in our lives, but if we hold on to our thoughts and emotions. We then keep the emotions and memories of harmful situations awake and present in our lives, we feed them and they occupy us. This gnaws at us and binds our energy. Assignments of guilt of all kinds are first-grade energy killers.

Our language also expresses the burden of unforgiveness:

- I bear enmity – I carry the burden.
- I am annoyed – the pathogenic reactions take place within me.
- I get an upset stomach – I get it.
  I take offence – who is taking the offence?

What is forgiving exactly?

Some people say: "Forgiving: yes. Forgetting: no." Yes, that is correct. Forgiving is not about forgetting what another person has done to me. We cannot forget that because everything we have ever experience, felt and thought is saved somewhere in our memory. On the contrary, if we forget we cannot forgive. Since our wounds and pains are saved somewhere, we must deal with the harmful experiences, look back and reappraise them. If we do not do this, we will not be healed. It would be highly counterproductive if we excused an inflicted harm by calling it a trifle or a bagatelle. You well know apologizing sentences such as these: "Oh, my mother did not really mean to say that, my father only acted like this because of his bad childhood, the times were hard, my husband was just quick-tempered, it was not that bad, it was not meant to hurt, let's forget it, I do not talk about such trifles, etc." No. Guilt remains guilt; and I cannot eliminate it by whitewashing it. This is how God sees it, by the way. He takes guilt so seriously that he gave his only Son and placed all sins onto him. And he forgives those who ask him for forgiveness because Jesus has died for our sins and has thus eliminated all our guilt in his representative suffering and death.

In the Greek language, the word forgiving originally has the sense of letting go, dismissing, releasing someone. It is a word of legal terminology: I release someone from his obligation to pay his debts to me. This step requires that I renounce to my rights, i.e., that I declare a waiver of my rights. This is an act of will and has nothing to do with my emotions. I need to release the other party and discharge them from the liability. Thus, I untie and release the fetter that has chained me to him or her. I no longer revolve around the "debtor's prison" or "guilt tower" and no longer need to guard, to observe, to feed or to judge my tormentor.

And what about my emotional wounds and the humiliations that continue to hurt me? They don't get healed by a simple act of will, do they? Yes, this is true, an act of will cannot heal the wounds, but it is the first step to healing.

In the following we will have a look at how humiliations and emotional wounds develop. Looking at our wounds is the first step on our way to forgiveness.

Humiliations and emotional wounds

We are hurt when our basic needs, i.e., love, appreciation, acceptance and safety, are not met. We are hurt by a lack of care, attention and confirmation, and by depreciating statements, comparisons and abuse of any kind. We are hurt most and deepest by the people who are closest to us, namely parents, siblings, friends, our partner, teachers and other important persons of authority.

As children, teenagers or young adults we are unable to cope with the humiliations of our closest reference persons; we can only suppress or push aside these humiliations. They block us and catch up with us until as we start to face them. We usually do not face them until our bodies have reacted with illnesses, and then we are forced to deal with them. Psychotherapy can help us, show correlations and explain behaviour patterns – but it cannot heal. Healing can only happen when we forgive, and we are dependent on God's help to forgive. The good news is that God loves to help us in that. The Gospel is that Jesus Christ wants to restore us. Deep humiliations have influence on our lives and put our self-esteem in danger. Only when we are willing to forgive, then a process of rethinking will begin. Only when we decide to release the guilt of others, then we will be able to accept ourselves as lovable and valuable persons, and we will accept and affirm our own lives. If we do not forgive, we will not only remain victims, but we will also become committers and offenders. A father or mother will subconsciously pass on the humiliations and wounds he or she has suffered. A long chain of guilt develops, going from great-grandparents to the great-grandchildren. But because God loves us, he sent Jesus Christ to eliminate the chain of guilt by forgiveness and by healing.

Steps: How to forgive

The most dangerous pains are those that we do not even want to think about because we are so afraid of facing the matter that had hurt us in the past. But it is essential that we finally mourn and grieve about what had happened to us. This is the first step on the way to forgiveness.

Sometimes we are so afraid of those wounds and the repeated pain that we bury these painful events deep down within us. The consequence is that we can no longer access them with our memory. These events have moved in our subconscious mind and we can no longer steer their effects. But our body reacts to humiliations and emotional pain on the long term. Watch out for physical feelings. If you feel pain ask yourself what may be behind it. Be honest with yourself.

It was very helpful for Hildegard to ask the Holy Spirit why she was suffering from severe arthritis. Initiated by the Holy Spirit she started a long process of looking back at her early childhood and reappraising it. A

Christian psychotherapist accompanied her and helped her to understand herself and the behaviour patterns that led to her illness.

Hildegard had to disconnect from the guilt that others had inflicted on her. Many of us need to do the same: Throw out the thoughts and the feelings that have wrongly settled down.

The three following practical instructions, given by a therapist, are very helpful:

1. I stop the self-talk that I repeatedly have with the offender.

2. I stop the revenge phantasies and self-pity attacks. Instead, I imagine that I throw the offender out – out of myself, out of my life, out of my house, and I lock the door.

3. I write down what has been done to me, because without a written complaint, a so-called "bill of indictment", there can neither be a conviction nor an acquittal. I imagine that the offender is seated on a chair in front of me. I read out loud the whole bill of indictment and tell them that I am disconnected from this guilt; I no longer have anything to do with it because Jesus has released me from it and has set me free.

King David is a role model for pouring out one's heart. We can read in the psalms how he has relieved his soul. Psalm 58 shows how he addressed the guilt that was inflicted on him (excerpts):

"Do you rulers indeed speak justly? Do you judge people with equity?
No, in your heart you devise injustice, and your hands mete out violence on the earth.
Even from birth the wicked go astray; from the womb they are wayward, spreading lies.
Break the teeth in their mouths, O God; Lord, tear out the fangs of those lions!
Let them vanish like water that flows away; when they draw the bow, let their arrows fall short.
May they be like a slug that melts away as it moves along.
Then people will say, 'Surely the righteous still are rewarded; surely there is a God who judges the earth.' "

Would you dare to say something alike when talking to God?

David had the ability and the habit to speak out before God what tormented him, so that the injustice inflicted on him and his own guilt would not poison him. Nowadays, most people are too morally adapted to do that. But we would like to strongly encourage you to read this psalm 58 in a modern translation and to then find your own words about your personal misfortune, your wounds and your offenders.

Forgiveness and current problems

The following paragraphs are about forgiveness in cases that do not refer to the past, but to the present, e.g., mobbing, inheritances or other current disputes.

Jesus himself has addressed injustice when the servant of the high priest beat him. Those who are afraid of addressing targeted provocations foster further aggressions. Those who let others do injustice to them without speaking out loud against them will lower the verge for the offenders to commit this injustice again. They will consequently have to cope with more and more humiliations. Mobbing victims are people who cannot and do not insist that they be respected and that their limits be observed. In order to insist on the respect of their limits, people need a sound self-esteem.

The apostle Paul had such self-esteem. In the Greek town of Philippi, he and his companion Silas were publicly beaten and sent to prison. Paul insisted on a public apology by the city council[51].

Surrender of guilt

Another instruction on how we can forgive comes originally from the bible; and the chief physician of a psychotherapist hospital has explained it in a very

---

[51] Acts 16:37-39

comprehensible way. He says we can surrender the whole legal matter to a higher legal authority. A surrender of the guilt is particularly appropriate when a victim wants to put an end to an unjustice in order to find peace and to set the healing process in motion.

A surrender of guilt means that the affected person hands over the punishment of the offender (i.e., their personal right for indemnification and compensation) to God. Thus, Jesus himself carries the guilt of the offender. This is what the bible calls forgiveness. Jesus himself eliminates thus the guilt that has been done to me. You might know that according to scientific studies, people who live in a close relationship with God can regain confidence that enables them to change and to endure in difficult life crises. These people can trust that God helps them in their crisis and that the crisis will finally work for their good.

Surrendering guilt will help with all emotional pains that happened in the past. It is not appropriate for our current relationships, such as marriage or partnerships, parent-child relationships or relationships at work or at church. In current situations, humiliations and harms have to be disclosed and addressed. It takes two people to reach reconciliation in a current situation because only then a clarification of the reasons and mutual forgiveness is possible.

Forgiving is a process

What has been said so far about the steps of forgiveness concerns our will, and not our emotions. We do not have much immediate influence on our feelings. A wise man once said: "You can send your own will by express courier, but your feelings will follow at a snail's pace." Forgiveness needs time. When we have not faced our emotional pains in years, our thoughts and emotions will have developed their own way. We need intensive training in order to retrain them to forgiving and to new thinking and behaviour patterns. We will need patience with ourselves in this rethinking and retraining process. We need to take many small steps and we will have to face and overcome backslides. Forgiving is often a painful, longsome process, and God will help us with it. We will need to repeat quite often that indeed, we have forgiven. And we will be rewarded in the end.

The "Midwest Institute for Forgiveness" was founded in the United States, and it has published the following research results[52]: Forgiving lowers blood pressure, soothes back-aches and depressions, supports rehabilitation after disc herniations (slipped vertebral disks) and helps fighting obesity that results from not being able to let go.

---

[52] Midwest Institute for Forgiveness and Newsweek, Sept 2004

Ms Eva Monzes, along with her twin sister, was subject to inhuman and cruel medical experiments during World War II in the concentration camp Ausschwitz. The experiments were carried out by surgeon Josef Mengele. Ms Monzes says in a newspaper article[53]:

„I plead for forgiving the offender because **it helps the victim to become healed**. It is not primarily about the offender! I think forgiveness is much better than justice, because justice does not help the victims. I have been asked whether I would have voted for a death sentence for Mr Mengele. But what would my gain have been? As a victim, justice and punishment of my offender do not help me much. Instead, the question about becoming healed is of major importance to me. I wanted to be able to visit Auschwitz one day and to go into a bar and dance the same evening. I refuse to play the role of the victim (editor's note: Jesus has already taken that role!). When I started to forgive, a burden fell off my shoulders that I had carried for almost 50 years. Forgiveness creates the opportunity for the victim to become somebody, to be a normal human being. A survivor has the right to forgive: the right to regain autonomy over his or her life."

---

[53] Frankfurter Rundschau (German newspaper) of 13.6.2003

Starting Points

In the following, we would like to suggest some starting points in case the seeking person does not bring forth any themselves.

These starting points shall by no means influence the Holy Spirit; they shall only serve as ideas where the seeking person might have got stuck.

Claims

Behind a symptom sometimes lies a claim of Satan[54]. A claim is a right of Satan to somebody or something. Satan did not have any claims on Jesus – Jesus said: "He has no hold over me[55]." But there might be claims that Satan has over us and that give him power. However, there are also positive claims, e.g., to the tree of life[56].

As long as a claim is not revealed and eliminated the symptoms will remain – because the enemy will not release anything that he is entitled to have.

The Holy Spirit is a great helper and reveals what hinders people in being set free. Here are a few examples (but there are, of course, many more):

- Family secrets such as alcohol problems, class conceits, greed, stinginess or sexual wrongdoings
- Curses
- Vows and oaths (also own vows such as "I will always be …, I will never be like my father…"). Oaths that our parents or ancestors had to take, e.g. on a political leader or in case of war.
- Abuse, abortion, trauma (the seeking person or their ancestors)

---

[54] Another name for Satan is "hinderer, adversary"; he can only hinder but not eliminate. Cf. Job 1:6.
[55] Joh 14:30b
[56] Revelation 22:14

- False accusations by parents, teachers, ourselves (I'm dumb; you will never be successful, etc.)
- Freemasonry and other secret societies

Corresponding biblical proof thereto:

Secrets
John 3:20: "Everyone who does evil hates the light, and will not come into the light for fear that their deeds will be exposed."

Ephesians 5:11-14: "Have nothing to do with the fruitless deeds of darkness, but rather expose them. It is shameful even to mention what the disobedient do in secret. But everything exposed by the light becomes visible—and everything that is illuminated becomes a light. This is why it is said: 'Wake up, sleeper, rise from the dead, and Christ will shine on you.' "

Curses
Revelation 22:3: "No longer will there be any curse. The throne of God and of the Lamb will be in the city, and his servants will serve him."

1 Samuel 3:13 et seqq.: Eli knew that his sons blasphemed God and thus contracted the curse.

Zechariah 5:3: "This is the curse that is going out over the whole land..."

Accusations
Matthew 5:22: "But I tell you that anyone who is angry with a brother or sister will be subject to judgment. Again, anyone who says to a brother or sister is answerable to the court. And anyone who says, 'You fool!' will be in danger of the fire of hell."

Ephesians 4:29: "Do not let any unwholesome talk come out of your mouths, but only what is helpful for building others up according to their needs, that it may benefit those who listen."

Claims based on actions or statements by ancestors
The person concerned either knows about it, then they can detach themself from it and the counsellor will cut sever the bonds and the claims in the name of Jesus. Or they do not know about it. In that case the counsellor will ask the Holy Spirit to show if there is a claim. The power of such claims can be effective through many generations.[57]

It is astounding that latest research proves that such claims and their negative effects are indeed transferred from one generation to the next, and that this transferred claim already takes effect during pregnancy.[58] We can see here how obvious the destructive power of sin is.

---

[57] Exodus 34:7
[58] Joachim Bauer, Das Gedächtnis des Körpers (the memory of the body), Piper publishing house, 19th edition, particularly chapters 6 and 14

Disburdening the heart

Another element of Hearing Counselling is that the seeking person disburdens their heart in the presence of a counsellor. It is necessary that the seeking person is prepared, and preparation needs time. It might make sense to set up another appointment.

Course of the session
The seeking person takes enough time to write everything down that comes to his/her mind, unsystematically and spontaneously: What grieves them, where do they feel treated unjustly, about what are they sad or mad, etc. This process can be compared to spilling out the contents of a lady's handbag: Everything just falls out. Later, the seeking person reads out loud to the counsellor/counselling team what they have written, if possible without shame and without omitting any of the points at the last second. During that time, the counsellor watches out and listens to the Holy Spirit if there are any points of importance:
- Accusations of the concerned person, by themself or by others
- Guilt inflicted to and by others
- Thoughts of fear, nightmares, wrong perceptions of God the Father, Jesus or the Holy Spirit.

The counsellor will pay attention to their own bodily feelings, because sometimes the Holy Spirit might talk through them.

Not everything that was written down is of importance, but the Holy Spirit will let the counsellor know what the key issues of the seeking person are. The counsellor will write down everything that the Holy Spirit draws to his attention; keywords might be enough. Then, the counsellor and the seeking person will discuss together what was written down, item by item. Generally, most points can be discussed quite quickly. We shall not be confused by their number, but shall discuss and treat all points of the unsystematic list one after the other:

- Break curses and accusations (own and by others), bring them to the cross of Jesus and bind them there for eternity.
- Replace wrong perceptions and conceptions by the right ones. Hereby, we speak to the spirit of the seeking person, not to the mind!
- Break the power of nightmares.
- Have the seeking person confess their sins and guilt, and then grant them forgiveness.
- When other people have become guilty towards the seeking person, the possibility of a "representative confession" might be considered. In any case, the power of the guilt shall be declared null and void: Jesus has already paid the price.
- Everything that comes into the light of Jesus loses its power.

During this process, we talk to the spirit of the person, not to the mind. The director of a baby hatch has made very good experiences when talking to the spirit of the new-born babies who were abandoned. Based on the findings of the French paediatrician and psychoanalyst, Françoise Dalto, she speaks out and proclaims God's truth to the babies (e.g., that he loves them, they are wanted), even though they cannot yet understand the words. We can proceed the same way. Sometimes, the spirit of the seeking person needs to be awakened or called into life, because it had no "right to exist" due to curses or negative determinations.

During the course of unburdening the heart, the seeking person can experience purification and cleansing in quite a short time frame. This cleansing is probably not comprehensive, and further steps to purification and cleansing can be taken (or repeated) at a later point in time when the Holy Spirit shows that this shall be done.

At the end of the session, the counsellor shall seal the seeking person with the Holy Spirit and anoints him/her if appropriate. Then, it shall be evaluated if the seeking person shall hand over his/her life to Jesus for the first or repeated time (including a confession of sins).

Time frame: mostly around 30 – 60 minutes.

Abuse (emotional, physical and spiritual)

Emotional abuse
In cases of emotional abuse, children had to serve as a replacement for a lost, absent or uncomprehending partner. They had to co-raise their siblings and lost their own childhood because responsibility was placed upon them that they were not able to carry at such an early age. Or they have burdened themselves with this responsibility (cf. chapter INCIDENTS, the example of the white elephant). In the name and by order of Jesus the responsibility is then taken off the person concerned.

Jesus did not burden anyone with responsibility. There are a few passages in the New Testament about "being responsible" in the sense of defending or justifying oneself,[59] but they are not about loading responsibility upon someone.

Physical/sexual abuse is to be handled with utmost care, and can generally not be solved in one counselling session. It is helpful to have several counsellors.

Three things are important.

First: The person concerned is to be told that God the Father was with him/her in that situation and has suffered with him/her. God himself will have to an-

---

[59] Acts 22:1; 1 Peter 3:15; Luke 12:11 and 21:14; Acts 19:33-40

swer the question to the person concerned why he did not prevent what had happened.

Second: Giving the inviolacy, restoring virginity back to the concerned person: "In the eyes of the Father you are now intact, unspoiled and pure, and nobody dare accuse you any more, neither others nor yourself. You are a prince/princess who has access to the throne of the Father. Nobody can reject you. You are no longer spoiled and dirty, but you are now purified and beautiful."

Third: The small child within the adult shall live. It may have its childhood. And it may live its childhood. God will compensate for what the devourer has stolen[60].

The Holy Spirit can show further and other things that shall be handled. He is incredibly creative, and his clues are tailored to the individual situation of the concerned person.

Another possibility that the Holy Spirit may show is that the body of the concerned person is given part by part to Jesus. Sometimes, the concerned person cannot continue speaking; in that case the counsellor shall ask the Holy Spirit what shall be done next.

An example of sexual abuse is given in the chapter INCIDENTS, "The bet".

---
[60] Joel 2:25

Spiritual abuse is understood as an abuse that spiritual leaders might perform. In their function as spiritual leaders they can misuse people in order to reach their own goals. These goals can be very positive, but the spiritual leaders have in that case neither listened to nor obeyed the Holy Spirit. They claim to know and to decide what is best for another person.

Persons of authority sometimes press their "sheep" (i.e., the people entrusted to their spiritual care) in a certain religious form, and this form often suffocates spiritual life. It is particularly suffocating when commandments and prohibitions are in the focus, rather than having a living relationship to the Father, to Jesus Christ and the Holy Spirit.

There is a great book by Watchman Nee, "The Latent Power of the Soul"[61]. The soul plays an important role in cases of spiritual abuse.

Typical statements of spiritual abuse are:
"The Lord has told me that you …"
"We are all called to mission in…"
"We need to donate more."
"You have to reach more people with the Gospel, whom did you tell about Jesus today?"

---

[61] Watchman Nee, The Latent Power of the Soul, Christian Fellowship Pub Inc. (June 1972)

The Holy Spirit often talks to us via others, but he never does that in an imperative tone or with a feeling of guilt or force.

Spiritual abuse might also take place when church life is extended to so many meetings per week that there is hardly time left for contacts to third parties (people not attending the church) and even for the own family.

Sometimes, a religious spirit hides behind that; and we are not able to discern that without the help of the Holy Spirit, because the difference is minimal. The satellite dish illustrates that very well: If there is a satellite dish on the roof, people on the street cannot see whether it is directed to ASTRA or to EUTELSAT; the deviation is minimal. But the effect is enormous, because in one case German programs are received, in the other case Southern European languages such as French and Italian.

A very good book about this topic is "Conquering the Religious Spirit" by Tommi Femrite[62].

---

[62] Tommi Femrite and Rebecca Wagner Sytsema, Conquering the Religious Spirit, Publisher: Chosen

Occult bonds

It might happen that occult bonds show during the Hearing Counselling session. In that case, the counsellor shall ask the Holy Spirit if such a bond really exists or if it is only pretended (we have already experienced the latter).

The causes for occult bonds can be traumatic experiences during which unclean spirits have gained access to the person. There might also be family bonds, or a conscious surrender to occult powers, or occult practices such as fortune-telling, reading palms, etc. (An occult bond might have occurred even if it has only been done for fun.) A gate for demonic powers might also have opened during anaesthesia, unconsciousness, freezing behaviour[63], a traumatic experience or when a loved one died or was severely hurt.

Where there is garbage, there are rats. Sometimes, the garbage (= sin) has to be eliminated first and then the rats (= the demonic powers); but sometimes it is the other way round. The Holy Spirit will show.

We do not want to go into more detail about occult bonds, but we recommend involving one or two experience counsellors if there is a concrete case.

---

[63] Lot's wife became a pillar of salt when she saw what happened in Sodom and Gomorrah (Genesis 19:26). Maybe she could not have lived on with what she saw and God had pity with her.

It is important that the spirits that were cast out are sent to the place that God assigns them. All synoptic report that Jesus allowed the spirits which he cast out of the demon-possessed man in the region of Gerasene to go into the herd of pigs.[64] Jesus himself points out that there shall be no empty room left void.[65] It is helpful to ask the Holy Spirit with what he would like to fill this purified room.

At the end, it makes sense to seal the seeking person in the name of the Father, the Son and the Holy Spirit.

An important bible passage for counsellors in the context of this topic says: "However, do not rejoice that the spirits submit to you, but rejoice that your names are written in heaven."[66]

Sin or guilt that I have committed or think I have committed

Abortion
Abortion is killing an unborn human being. The seeking person asks for forgiveness and the counsellor will grant forgiveness in the name of Jesus. It is important to declare with words to lay the aborted child into the Father's arms or lap. God wanted this child, and it will now wait in heaven for its parents.

---

[64] Luke 8:28-33
[65] Luke 11:24-26
[66] Luke 10:20

Miscarriage

We need the Holy Spirit to show whether there is guilt or not. In the book „Heaven is for real" there is a wonderful story about miscarriage: In heaven, the little boy meets his nameless sister and later tells his parents about the encounter. This takes away the pain from his mother and father, and converts it into anticipation.[67].

Example - Michelle:

When praying, Hildegard had a vision for Michelle that showed a baby in a golden dress, laying on the Father's lap and being held by him. Michelle started to cry and when she was able to speak again, she told about a miscarriage she had at a very late stage of pregnancy. This vision of the baby on the Father's lap has freed Michelle from her deep sadness.

Attitude or measures of self-protection

The hurt child within us sometimes had to establish self-protection measures in order to survive. These measures used to be helpful, but have now turned into obstacles and blockades for our develop-ment.

Pride

Pride can be found in sentences and self-accusations such as: "I can do it all by myself. I do not trust any-body. I will not be fooled." Generally, pride is con-nected with a high willingness to perform and with the inability to ask for help or to accept help. Perfec-

---

[67] Todd Burpo, Heaven is for real, Thomas Nelson edition, 2012

tionism can be a form of pride. Pride can also show in irony, in cool and distanced relationships or in an isolated way of life. The cause is mostly a deep loss of trust in the early childhood.

Escape
We hereby mean the escape from one's own fears, problems and abysses into addictions of all kind: alcohol, shopping, eating, illnesses, depressions, Internet/computer, new media, Facebook and other social networks, denial to take part in real life.

Rebellion
Passive (also called depressive) rebellion is expressed in a "no" to the life that God gave me. Passive rebellion results in self-pity, escape into the role of the victim, escape into depression – the rebellion is aimed at one's own heart. Active rebellion is expressed in defiance, offence, aggression, dissatisfaction, demands, control, refusal, hate and even murderous thoughts.

Fear
Fear has a lot of forms, such as feeling limited or distressed, fear of making mistakes, fear of failure, fear to come short, fear of refusal and exclusion. Fear thus turns into a prison for us.

Shame
We hereby mean false shame about our hurt heart, our history and our wounds. We hide our heart and carry masks, we produce lies such as "my parents could not help it; it was not meant that way; my husband could not act in a different way".

Depression
Depression is a mental dysfunction or psychic disorder with states of mental dejectedness or melancholy. It can be described as an aggression against oneself (escape).

Aggression
Aggression can be caused by negative feelings and can be expressed against the offender in thoughts, feelings and also in actions.

The counsellor can ask the Holy Spirit to show the protective measures that the seeking person has established. Self-protection measures are very persistent, tenacious, and deeply anchored in one's behaviour and still work after a person has given their life to Jesus. They prevent people from further development.

Sexual misconduct

In our society and in individual lives we can see the damage caused by sexual misconduct. According to biblical understanding, every sexual relationship establishes a unification of body, soul and spirit of the persons involved[68]. But who can become a unity with several or even dozens of people? This inevitably leads to disruption.

The Holy Spirit can show how the damage can be healed. The story of the Samaritan woman shows the approach that Jesus used. Jesus saw the damages she had suffered from her changing relationships. But he did not condemn her and he did not even ask her to repent. To him, the encounter and relationship with her were far more important, because in a relationship, changing and healing will grow – and not from our own efforts.

We have the impression that sexual misconduct is overemphasized in some churches. This probably happens because the media drowns us with sex. Jesus preached a lot more about greediness, idolatry, money, envy and pride. Sexual misconduct might be so over-emphasized because it is more visible than envy or pride, e.g., when two people who are not married move together in one apartment. Greediness and pride can be embellished in a Christian way. We

---

[68] Genesis 2:24: They become ONE flesh.

should beware of condemning people – the Holy Spirit sees them in another light than we do!

There is no hierarchy of sin; there are no very small sins on one side and very evil sins on the other side. Yes, there is the sin of blasphemy against the Spirit[69] of which Jesus says that it cannot be forgiven. In Hebrews[70] we find the following bible passage:
"It is impossible for those who have once been enlightened, who have tasted the heavenly gift, who have shared in the Holy Spirit, who have tasted the goodness of the word of God and the powers of the coming age and who have fallen away, to be brought back to repentance. To their loss they are crucifying the Son of God all over again and subjecting him to public disgrace."

These verses surely do not refer to sexual misconduct. Every sin separates us from God and does damage to us, no matter if we believe that or not.

---

[69] Matthew 12:31 and Mark 3:29
[70] Hebrews 6: 4-6

Practical Tips and Tools

There is no universal method for Hearing Counselling. Every hearing counsellor is absolutely dependent upon the talking and the guidance of the Holy Spirit. There is no substitute for him; no experience and no education can ever replace the "know-how" of the Holy Spirit with his wisdom and experience of thousands of years and millions of God's children.

On the other hand, there are tools and spiritual weapons we can take "out of a toolbox" when the Holy Spirit wants us to use them.

According to 2 Corinthians 6:7 the weapons are divided into two categories: There are weapons to the left and weapons to the right; meaning weapons for defence and weapons for offence.

The way we see it, the following two weapons serve for defence:

1. The armour of God, according to Ephesians 6:11-18a
   - The helmet of salvation that holds our thoughts with the Holy Spirit.
   - The belt of truth that prevents the garment (or tunic) from flattering, which would make us stumble when we go forward.

- The feet fitted with readiness that comes from the gospel of peace (i.e., that the Father has mercy with his children).
- The large shield of faith (= trust in Jesus and in the Holy Spirit) that completely covers us, protects us and wards off aggressions that indeed happen. Aggressions to the seeking person could be that he/she is blocked or silent or wants to run away.
- The sword of the Spirit, which is the word of God, is actually a weapon of offence, but Jesus used it as a defence weapon when he was tempted by Satan by saying: "It is written…"[71]

According to Ephesians 6:17 the Holy Spirit gives us the "sword of the word of God".

2. We place ourselves under the protection of the blood of Jesus, under the protection of the Highest.
We have made pretty good experiences with (verbally) placing us, the seeking person, our families and our possessions under the blood of Jesus at the beginning of every counselling session. We do that so the enemy will not have access or influence, neither on us, nor on our thoughts, nor on our spirit who is talking with the Holy Spirit.

---

[71] Luke 4:4+8+12

Biblical proof taken from the Old Testament

Exodus 12:13
When the Israelites left Egypt, the blood of the pessach lamb protected their firstborns from dying.

Psalm 91:1-2
"Whoever dwells in the shelter of the Most High will rest in the shadow of the Almighty.
I will say of the Lord, 'He is my refuge and my fortress, my God, in whom I trust.' "

Biblical proof taken from the New Testament

John 6:53
"Jesus said to them, 'Very truly I tell you, unless you eat the flesh of the Son of Man and drink his blood, you have no life in you.' "
This exceeds by far the act of "placing ourselves under the blood of Jesus" and surely means the Lord's Supper. The blood of Jesus creates life and maintains life; this is the deeper sense of these words.

Ephesians 2:13
"But now in Christ Jesus you who once were far away have been brought near by the blood of Christ."

Hebrews 2:14
"Since the children have flesh and blood, he too shared in their humanity so that by his death he might break the power of him who holds the power of death—that is, the devil."

Hebrews 12:22-24

"But you have come to Mount Zion, to the city of the living God, the heavenly Jerusalem. You have come to thousands upon thousands of angels in joyful assembly, to the church of the firstborn, whose names are written in heaven. You have come to God, the Judge of all, to the spirits of the righteous made perfect, to Jesus the mediator of a new covenant, and to the sprinkled blood that speaks a better word than the blood of Abel."

This is a reference to the last plague in Egypt when applying the blood of a faultless lamb (hint to Jesus) onto the doorposts (i.e., the entrance in the house with the whole family and all possessions) made the angel of death pass by.

Hebrews 13:12

"And so Jesus also suffered outside the city gate to make the people holy through his own blood."

1 Peter 1:1-2

"Peter, an apostle of Jesus Christ, to God's elect, exiles scattered throughout the provinces of Pontus, Galatia, Cappadocia, Asia and Bithynia, who have been chosen according to the foreknowledge of God the Father, through the sanctifying work of the Spirit, to be obedient to Jesus Christ and sprinkled with his blood: Grace and peace be yours in abundance."

Revelation 7:14

"I answered, 'Sir, you know.' And he said, 'These are they who have come out of the great tribulation; they have washed their robes and made them white in the blood of the Lamb.' "

The spiritual weapons of offence are the practical tips and tools outlined in this chapter. Possibly, there are further tools, especially in the realms of physical healing, into which the Holy Spirit has only introduced us very little. Jesus has explicitly given us the order[72]: "Heal the sick, raise the dead, cleanse those who have leprosy, drive out demons. Freely you have received; freely give."

The double-edged sword

Psalm 149, verses 6 and 9
The double-edged sword consists of
- Worship in the mouth/on the lips (verse 6) and
- Carrying out the sentence written against them (verse 9).

Thereto we need to know the verdict and we need to give God all honour, because it is God who acts – we cannot do it. We need to know which verdict the Holy Spirit has pronounced and how we shall carry it out under his instruction. The worship on our lips means that all honour belongs to God, and not to us or our own wisdom or experience.

---

[72] Matthew 10:8

The double-edged sword divides joint and marrow[73], meaning soul and spirit. It divides that what comes from God from those things that do not come from God. In specific situations, we often cannot clearly discern what is good and appropriate and what it not. The Holy Spirit can help us here with a bible passage or by defining the situation with a precise word, by distinguishing between spirits or by revealing something that we cannot know, e.g., the name of an evil spirit that holds the person imprisoned, or an event of the past.

Carrying out the verdict means to separate the person who belongs to God from what is not from God: "I separate from you by order and authority of Jesus this behaviour, this evil spirit ..." or "I separate from you by order and authority of Jesus the connection and bond to this person."

The room that has been emptied must be filled with what the Holy Spirit gives us for the seeking person: the shalom peace of the Father, the love of the Father, Jesus's mercy, the fruit of the Spirit ...

Example:
Casting out a religious spirit

Four persons were present at a hearing counselling session: The counsellors A, B and C and the seeking

---

[73] Hebrews 4:12

person S. At the beginning, all placed themselves under the protection of the blood of Jesus.

B had the first impression as a vision: A spirit of money. This bond was released.

Then, the impression of a dazzling, ever-changing spirit came up. We continued to ask the Holy Spirit what to do next. The impression came up that there was another spirit.

But we needed the name of the spirit to cast it out. We asked the spirit to reveal its name (biblical proof for this is in Luke 8, 30 when Jesus asks for the name of the spirit), but the spirit did not react to this request. Then we asked the Holy Spirit to help us. After some questioning, A and B knew **exactly** at the same second the name of the spirit, B pronounced it and A confirmed it. This bond was also released.

Then, S started to defend himself with many words that he wanted justice only based on biblical proof, and that this could not be wrong. When one counsellor mentioned that also Satan uses the bible, S tried to refute this with many words, saying that in this case no one could trust the bible and that every promise of God would be invalid. But this was not what the counsellor had said. Two counsellors had the impression that it was about a religious spirit, and they said so.

S then pronounced a long prayer of cancellation. But nothing happened. The religious spirit had attached itself to the statement that Satan does not belong to God's side, and this is the truth.

The Holy Spirit then gave the counsellors unity and the impression that it was indeed a religious spirit. But how to cast it out when S defended it still? S defended the religious spirit with quotations from the bible and conclusions that were not entirely correct. The discussions continued, but led to the same question: How to show to S that it was a religious spirit that ostensibly defended the bible, but that in truth led back to the law and to self-redemption?

The spirit revealed itself in a casual remark about fishing: "when the fish fidgets on a hook..." (When Jesus and the disciples cast a net on the Lake of Galilee). This remark caught B's attention, and the counsellors got the idea how to explain the situation to S: The fish is caught on a hook (i.e., the spirit has caught possession of the human being). Because it is a barbed hook, the hook cannot be loosened easily. The religious rage of S was like a barbed hook, he defended his view angrily. As long as S did not give up his point of view, the spirit would not leave.

S understood that the religious spirit had unperceivedly gained access to him, and that was why S had these fits of rage in questions concerning his faith.

But what was the spirit's name? B's first definition was "anti-love" and then C stated: "hate". Now, the separation from S and the spirit could be initiated, using the sword of the word of God that separates joint and marrow. The counsellors were able to separate the religious spirit from the true Spirit of God; they bound it and cast it out.

During that process, S confessed another spirit. It was also cast out and sent to the place that Jesus assigned it for eternity.

During the following blessing, S was blessed with the words that "the real S" would now emerge, just like the Father had created him and meant him to be.

In this case, it was very helpful that several counsellors were present who complemented one another. When one of them did not know how to proceed further, the other stepped in. The counsellors could agree by eye contact if they were on the right track, and they were able to introduce new arguments or impressions into the discussion.

On the next day, the counsellors pronounced a blessing prayer over S: All insinuations that the religious spirit had given to S (and that had caused the stereotypical long bible quotations) were erased.

Touching and hugging

The counsellors should ask the seeking person beforehand if it is OK to touch or hug them. The Holy Spirit will lead the counsellors in this decision, too. Sometimes, people (not only women, but also men) long to be hugged, without any further intentions. Nowadays, this is not easy (see "About Hearing").

The Touch Research Institute (TRI) in Miami/USA investigates how important physical touch is, and they found: new-born babies grow and develop faster when they are touched and given massages, the memory of Alzheimer patients improves, and the immune system of HIV patients gets stronger. Via the touch of another person, a human being can recognize themselves.

We had counselling sessions that consisted of 50% in hugging the seeking person, letting them cry or just rest in our arms, like in the lap of Abraham or rather in the lap of the Father. Couple therapist Wolfgang Schmidbauer says: "Many people are so hurt on the inside that they think: Whoever touches me so deeply must love me deeply."

However, it is important not to give only human warmth, but to do what the Holy Spirit tells us to do. Sometimes, it is about loving the seeking persons like a child, to tell them what the Father, Abba, wants to tell them, to hug them like a baby. Sometimes, they want to cry and shout out everything that has been done to them. Sometimes, they want to be hugged while shouting out their anger at the same time. Sometimes, they want to drum on the chest of the counsellor and cry out their anger.

And they may still want to experience the blessing later on, when the counsellor lays a blessing hand on them. Or they may want to be hugged tightly before leaving, as if the counsellor would tell them: "It is good from God's point of view; you are good in his eyes."

It is important that we do not align the seeking person to us, but that they focuse on what Jesus and the Father have for them. We are only human beings, and sooner or later people might be disappointed by us.

Example:
The family secret
Anne came to us because she suffered from the fact that her father ignored her. She told us about his birthdays. She had a birthday present for him but did not dare to give it to him out or fear of rejection. When she dared to give it to him in the evening, he said harshly: "Now, I don't need any more, it's late." She told us more hurtful events, but we had the impression that this was not the root of the problem.

When we listened closely to the Holy Spirit again, we saw a picture of a tightly shut mouth, meaning forced silence.

Then, the horrible family history started to break out: suicides, threatening of suicide, and the forced silence about them. The father told his daughter something that the mother must not know because it would kill her since she had a weak health. And the mother told her daughter things that the father must not know. All of the five siblings had secrets that they were forced to keep and that they must not babble out accidentally.

When Anne remembered what her grandmother said, it turned out that these family secrets already existed for generations. These secrets had the effect that Anne did not trust anybody because she never knew if something was hidden from her.

Before she was able to forgive she had to let her anger out. In Heinrich's arms, she drummed at his chest and shouted out her accusations.

We finally confessed to Jesus the whole situation as guilt. In place of her father and her mother, we asked Anne for forgiveness, and we cancelled the bonds of the generations. We blessed Anne with renewed trust. We removed the yoke for her mother off of her shoulders, and then we placed the light yoke of Jesus on her. Since then, every time that someone tries to put a new yoke (i.e., a new responsibility or burden) onto Anne, she declares that she already bears a yoke: the light and loving yoke of Jesus.

Cancelling, setting free, releasing, and taking off the burden.

We hereby talk about
- cancelling and breaking free of bonds,
- declaring curses as void,
- cutting off dependencies,
- taking off burdens that people do not have to carry, regardless if other people had loaded the burden on them or if they did it themselves.

While hearing, the Holy Spirit will show what it is about in every single case. What we will do then is an active process. We might declare:
"In the name and by order of our Lord Jesus I release you from the guilt of your ancestors (e.g., of sins during war time).
"I declare all false accusations for void that your parents/teachers/... have spoken over you."
"I take the burden off you that people have wrongly loaded upon you/that you have loaded onto yourself."

**Biblical proof:
Releasing, setting free**

Psalm 10:19-20
"The Lord looked down from his sanctuary on high, from heaven he viewed the earth, to hear the groans of the prisoners and release those condemned to death."

Psalm 116:16
"… you have freed me from my chains."

Psalm 146
V5: "Blessed are those, whose help is the God of Jacob, whose hope is in the Lord their God."
V7: "He upholds the cause of the oppressed and gives food to the hungry. The Lord sets prisoners free."
V9: "The Lord watches over the foreigner and sustains the fatherless and the widow." (Those who live without husband or parents – even if they are still alive)

Isaiah 58:6
"Is not this the kind of fasting I have chosen: to lose the chains of injustice and untie the cords of the yoke, to set the oppressed free and break every yoke?"

Jeremiah 40:4
"But today I am freeing you from the chains on your wrists."

Releasing and redeeming

Isaiah 52:2-3
"Shake off your dust; rise up, sit enthroned, Jerusalem. Free yourself from the chains on your neck, Daughter Zion, now a captive. For this is what the Lord says: 'You were sold for nothing, and without money you will be redeemed.' "

Isaiah 61:1-2
"The Spirit of the Sovereign Lord is on me, because the Lord has anointed me to proclaim good news to the poor. He has sent me to bind up the brokenhearted, to proclaim freedom for the captives and release from darkness for the prisoners, to proclaim the year of the Lord's favour …"

Matthew 18:18
"Truly I tell you, whatever you bind on earth will be bound in heaven, and whatever you loose on earth will be loosed in heaven."

Mark 7:35
"At this, the man's ears were opened; his tongue was loosened and began to speak plainly."

Luke 13
V 11: "And a woman was there who had been crippled by a spirit for eighteen years. She was bent over and could not straighten up at all."
V 12: "When Jesus saw her, he called her forward and said to her, 'Woman, you are set free from your infirmity.' "
V 16: "Then should not this woman, a daughter of Abraham, whom Satan has kept bound for eighteen long years, be set free on the Sabbath day from what bound her?"

Galatians 3:13
"Christ redeemed us from the curse of the law by becoming a curse for us, for it is written: 'Cursed is everyone who is hung on a pole.' "

Luke 11:21-22
"When a strong man, fully armed, guards his own house, his possessions are safe. But when someone stronger attacks and overpowers him, he takes away the armor in which the man trusted and divides up his plunder."

Matthew 12:22-27   (also Mark 3:22 et seqq.)
A demon-possessed man is healed and the Pharisees claim that Jesus did that by a covenant with the highest of the demons.
V 28: "But if it is by the Spirit of God that I drive out demons, then the kingdom of God has come upon you."
V 29: "Or again, how can anyone enter a strong man's house and carry off his possessions unless he first ties up the strong man? Then he can plunder his house."

Releasing, setting free from burdens
Psalm 55:22
"Cast your cares on the Lord and he will sustain you."

Psalm 81:5b-7
"I heard an unknown voice say: 'I removed the burden from their shoulders; their hands were set free from the basket. In your distress you called and I rescued you.' "

Isaiah 9:2-4
V 2: "The people walking in darkness have seen a great light... "
V 3: "You have enlarged the nation and increased their joy; they rejoice before you as people rejoice at the harvest, as warriors rejoice when dividing the plunder."
V 4: "For as in the day of Midian's defeat, you have shattered the yoke that burdens them, the bar across their shoulders, the rod of their oppressor."
(cf. Judges 7)

Isaiah 22:25
"In that day," declares the Lord Almighty, "the peg driven into the firm place will give way; it will be sheared off and will fall, and the load hanging on it will be cut down." The Lord has spoken.

Matthew 11:30
"For my yoke is easy and my burden is light."

Freedom, healing

Luke 4:18 (quotation from Jes 61:1-2 and 58: 6)
"The Spirit of the Lord is on me, because he has anointed me to proclaim good news to the poor. He has sent me to proclaim freedom for the prisoners and recovery of sight for the blind, to set the oppressed free."

Matthew 10:1
"Jesus called his twelve disciples to him and gave them authority to drive out impure spirits and to heal every disease and sickness."

Casting out demons

Some verses from the New Testament

Mark 16:17
"In my name they will drive out demons …"

Mark 3:14-15
"He (Jesus) appointed twelve that they might be with him and that he might send them out to preach and to have authority to drive out demons."

Mark 6:13
"They drove out many demons and anointed many sick people with oil and healed them."

Setting free

Hebrews 2:15
"… and (Jesus could) free those who all their lives were held in slavery by their fear of death."

Psalm 18
V 19: "He brought me out into a spacious place; he rescued me because he delighted in me."

V 47-48: "He is the God who avenges me, who subdues nations under me, who saves me from my enemies. You exalted me above my foes; from a violent man you rescued me."

Jeremiah 15:21
"I will save you from the hands of the wicked and deliver you from the grasp of the cruel."

Fear

Leviticus 26:36
Guilt can be the reason for fear.

After cancelling/releasing
It is important to (verbally) cut all bonds and to ask the Holy Spirit that he seals all open areas. Please see the point "Anointing" in this chapter.

Here are a few issues of major importance for Muslims who have given their lives to Jesus:
- Renouncing from RAMADAN (that includes fasting and the subsequent binding blood sacrifice)
- Renouncing from the prayer FATIHA that contains an oath to Mohammed and his helpers.
- Breaking the sentences and oaths that were declared during pregnancy and after birth, especially over male babies. Also girls need to be released from them.

Example:
Fear in the house

Due to a job change, Sonia and her family planned to move to another city where they had already rented a house. Sonia had panical fear that someone would break into that house.

We asked the Holy Spirit for direction. Hildegard received a question: Are there situations in your life when you opened the door of your heart and when fear entered?

The Holy Spirit then reminded Sonia about two incidents of her past:

During her studies, Sonia was once followed by a man at night and just managed to shut the door before the man could reach the door handle. Heinrich expressed a representative confession of guilt for the man and asked Sonia for forgiveness. Sonia was able to forgive the man, and joy could be seen on her face.

A second incident happened when Sonia shared an apartment with other people. One night, all of them woke up when they heard a woman crying out loud on the street. They were very scared and asked the boyfriend of one of the girls to have a look outside – but it seemed that the matter had already been settled.

The Holy Spirit showed us that in this moment of shock, a spirit of fear had gained access to Sonia. We cast it out in the name of Jesus and ordered it to go to the place that Jesus assigned it. Sonia was relieved.

Then, Sonia remembered an incident when she wanted to break up with her former boyfriend; she had been very unsure whether he would get violent – but this did not happen. We thanked God for her protection.

Finally, the cause of her fear turned out to be a fear of her mother. A relative had a second set of keys to the house they lived in, and he laid claim on the house. Therefore, Sonia had always felt unsafe during her childhood and adolescence.

We set Sonia free from the fear of her mother, and replaced the fear by Jesus' love for her.

At last, her fears vanished.

Anointing with oil

When the Holy Spirit has strongly intervened in the life of a seeking person, the counsellors can anoint them at the end of the counselling session.

There are many ways of anointing, here are some examples:

Anointing with (fragrant) oil, e.g., anointing oil from Israel, or plain olive oil (antiallergenic), or a mix of jojoba oil with a small part of rose oil.

The counsellors can draw three crosses on the person's forehead and say: "I now seal what has happened in the name of the Father (draw 1st cross, with oil applied on the finger), in the name of the Son (draw 2nd cross) and in the name of the Holy Spirit (draw 3rd cross). Nobody can ever change that forevermore. Amen."

The counsellor can also draw a cross into the palms and say: "I now anoint these hands to do ..." (depending on what the Holy Spirit said).

The same applies to the feet: "I anoint these feet that they walk on the new path that the Holy Spirit has shown."

Biblical proof for anointing can be found in James 5:14; that especially applies after a confession of sin.

In the Old Testament, anointing is often a sign for the king[74], and we are the King's children indeed.

When priests are dedicated, they also are anointed with oil[75], and in the sense of the New Testament we are priests, too.

We can also anoint people with oil when they are weak[76], we can anoint for cleansing[77], healing of the sick[78] and for certain tasks[79].

Intercession or the representative confession of guilt

According to our experiences, intercession or the representative confession of guilt is one of the most effective weapons to destroy Satan's strongholds. John Paul Jackson writes: Repentance is our strongest weapon for fighting[80]. But we need the Holy Spirit to make clear when, where and how to do it.

---

[74] 1 Samuel 9:16; 2 Samuel 2:4; 1 Kings 1:39; 2 Kings 23:30
[75] Exodus 28:41; Leviticus 8:12
[76] 2 Chronicles 28:15
[77] Ezekiel 16:9
[78] Mark 6:13; Revelation 3:18 in fig. sense
[79] Matthew 26:7; Luke 7:38; John 12:3
[80] John Paul Jackson, Needless Casualties of War, Kingsway Communications Ltd, 2000.

Definition
In the place of and thus representing the mother/father/teacher/boss/tormentor ... , the counsellor asks the seeking person for forgiveness for what had been done to them. First, the counsellor shall express the confession of the guilt that was committed; it shall not be an explanation or excuse. Then, they shall ask for forgiveness and express the regret about the effects that the guilt had in the life of the seeking person. The Holy Spirit will help to find the right words and he often gives more impulses on what do say additionally.

It is necessary that the seeking person names the guilt upfront and in detail; that they define what has been done to them and what they felt (see chapter "Forgiveness"). If the seeking person has difficulties to express these deeds, the counsellor can help with questions or can pre-define sentences.

Important: It is not about rational explanations (why, wherefore), but it is about setting up a "bill of indictment", a complaint that includes pronouncing the guilt. At this stage, no comprehension for the tormentor shall be given ("But he could not act differently because ...", and alike).

It is often advisable to give the seeking person enough time to write down this bill of indictment. Only then they will be able to separate from the guilt committed to them. This is important because if a person does not remember what they experienced or what happened to them and if this does not come to light, then they cannot let go. The seeking person must learn to name the guilt. Without indictment or accusation there will be no judgement and no thus acquittal.

According to our experience it is very helpful when two counsellors are present, ideally one man and one woman. The male counsellor shall representatively confess the guilt of a man, and the female counsellor of a woman, and they shall declare it face-to-face with the seeking person (and with Jesus). After that, the other counsellor will pronounce forgiveness for tormentor – in the name and by order of Jesus, and the effects of the guilt are declared null and void. We are not entitled to judge if the tormentor deserved acquittal of their guilt because Jesus has forgiven us our sins, too. The weight of the guilt does not matter. The counsellor will testify: The guilt exists no longer.

Biblical proof

1. Genesis 50:15-17
   Joseph's father and brothers send a messenger unto Joseph, confessing their guilt towards him and asking for his forgiveness.
2. Exodus 32:30-33
   Moses asks God for forgiveness – in place of the people of Israel.

3. Leviticus 16:20-22
   When the High Priest has confessed all sins of the

people of Israel (in place of them) he loaded these sins on a goat and released it in the wilderness.

4. Leviticus 26:40 and Nehemia 9:2
   The people proclaim their (own) sins and the sins of their ancestors.

5. Numeri 14:19
   Moses asks God, in place of the people of Israel, for forgiveness of their sins.

6. Nehemia 1:6
   Nehemia confesses the sins of the people of Israel.

7. Three times in chapter 9:
   Esra 9, Nehemia 9, Daniel 9
   Esra confesses the sins of the mixed marriages.
   In Nehemia 9:16 et seqq., the Levites (named in verses 4 and 5) confess the guilt of the forefathers.
   Daniel 9: Daniel prays in lieu of the people of Israel and confesses their sins. The archangel Gabriel comes to give him the right insight and understanding (!).

8. 1 Samuel 25:23-32
   Abigail takes on the guilt of her husband Nabal.

9. Jeremiah 14:20
   Jeremiah and the people acknowledge the guilt of their ancestors.

10. Ezekiel 22:30
 God seeks people who stand before him in the gap (of guilt).

11. Jesus **carries** the sin in lieu of us; he did not only confess it (cf. Luke 23:34).

12. Romans 9:2-3
 "I have great sorrow and unceasing anguish in my heart. For I could wish that I myself were cursed and cut off from Christ for the sake of my people, those of my own race."

13. James 5:16
 "Therefore confess your sins to each other and pray for each other so that you may be healed. The prayer of a righteous person is powerful and effective."

14. John 20:19-23
 We would like to explain this bible passage in detail. Jesus came into the midst of his disciples for the first time after his resurrection on Easter Sunday, only Thomas was missing.
 "Peace be with you!"
 These were his first words. Then he identifies himself, he shows them his pierced hands and his side. The disciples rejoice.

"Peace be with you!", Jesus says for the second time.
Peace is his intention, his plan and his threefold assignment. Peace for us and for those to whom we reach out.

1. The reason for the mission:
"As the Father has sent me, I am sending you." He explains in verse 17 who the Father is:
"I am ascending **to my Father and your Father**, to my God and your God."
The mission is explained before in the Gospel of John[81]: With the same authority with which God sends Jesus, Jesus sends his disciples. This is an assignment, a mission – and not a responsibility (see chapter "About Hearing"). We are messengers and ambassadors, but Jesus and the Father have the responsibility.

2. The companion in this mission:
"And with that he breathed on them and said 'Receive the Holy Spirit.'" Another translation of the word "to breathe" from Greek language is "to blow into".
When we hear this, we remember Genesis 2:7:
"Then the Lord God formed a man from the dust of the ground and breathed into his nostrils the breath of life, and the man became a living being."
It is about something alive, a lively relationship; it is not about precisely following the letters of the

---

[81] John 12:49-50

law. A new type emerges: the human being filled with the Holy Spirit. Jesus spoke of that when talking to Nicodemus (being born again, born of the Spirit, the new man).

3. Authority to forgive sins:
"If you forgive anyone's sins, their sins are forgiven; if you do not forgive them, they are not forgiven."
Jesus says, this is my mission for you, and I have given you a counsellor, I have blown my counsellor into you, and you shall listen to him. I trust you that you will do it right.
Jesus does not mention any prerequisites except listening to the Holy Spirit. No well-phrased confessions, no signs of deep sorrow; and the person whom we forgive does not even have to be present or alive.
That is a wonderful opportunity to create peace, under the authority of Jesus Christ.
If you do so (in Greek language the verb "forgive" stands in the subjunctive form), then the person is forgiven. **If** you do so, then forgiveness takes effect **now** and it lasts forever.
We personally believe and have experienced that "standing in the gap" and the representative confession of guilt is a wonderful opportunity to follow the mission of Christ.

But it goes even further:
"… if you do not forgive them, they are not forgiven."

In the English Standard Version, it says: "... if you withhold forgiveness from any, it is withheld."
That means, if we as Jesus's disciples do NOT forgive someone, if we withhold and do not bring the guilt that the Holy Spirit has revealed to the cross, then the guilty person remains guilty, even though the seeking, tormented person has for-given the tormentor.

It is our decision to forgive the initiator of the sin in the name of Jesus. Do we really see the scope of this decision?

With the help of the Holy Spirit we can see what Jesus has entrusted us with.

This picture illustrates the scope and the context:

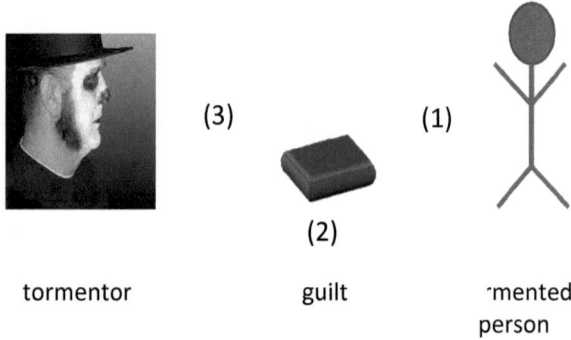

tormentor   guilt   ˉmented person

When the tormented person forgives they cut the bond that binds to the tormentor at position (1).

But the guilt (2) remains. The representative confession of guilt by the counsellor goes one step further and asks Jesus to forgive the tormentor's guilt, and carries it to the cross.

The approach of the representative confession of guilt addresses all three positions: forgiveness by the tormented person (1), forgiveness of the deed (2) and forgiveness of the guilt of the tormentor (3). This means to stand in the gap. Even if the tormentor does not see it that way or is no longer alive. Nobody can ever accuse the tormentor before God for this deed anymore! As described in Job 1:9-11 or in Revelation 12:10b. Jesus carried all the sin of the world that we have confessed to him (directly and as a representative), therefore this sin is disposed of once and for all.

This effect can be noticed and experienced in the visible and in the invisible world. We might feel that this is unjust – the guilt of the tormentor is erased! Nobody can ever accuse them before God any more.

But didn't Jesus do the same with my guilt? He erased it.

You may say: „Yes, but my guilt was not as wicked."
The question is: "Does that matter – or don't you rather prefer to be free?"

Ezekiel 22:30 shows us what the representative confession of guilt actually is: Standing in the breach or stepping into the gap before God.

Several bible passages in the Old Testament show that.

2 Kings 12:5 et seqq.
King Joash notices that the temple (note: we are the temple of the Holy Spirit[82]) has gaps and takes the tasks of preservation of the temple from the priests, he creates a source of income and hires people who act in good faith.

Nehemia 6:1 et seqq.
Nehemia is busy removing the gaps and rebuilding the wall in the destroyed city of Jerusalem; that is such an important task that he is indispensable for other duties.

Isaiah 22:9
Grief expressed before God about damaged parts in the wall.

Isaiah 30:12-13
"… this sin will become for you like a high wall, cracked and bulging." Guilt is like a crack in our "wall of faith".

---

[82] 1 Corinthians 3:16 and 6:19

Isaiah 58:12
A name of honour is: Repairer of Broken Walls.

Ezekiel 13:5
"You have not gone up to the breaches in the wall to repair it for the people of Israel so that it will stand firm in the battle on the day of the Lord".

Ezekiel 22:30
"I looked for someone among them who would build up the wall and stand before me in the gap on behalf of the land so I would not have to destroy it, but I found no one."

Example:
The double backpack

We were sitting together with a few people one evening during a weekend seminar and discussed about how to get rid of burdens. Conny mentioned a "double backpack", but then the discussions turned another way.

On Saturday, Heinrich and Conny took a walk together and Conny told him about her loving, believing grandmother and also about the abuse of a relative to whom she and her siblings went during daytime when their mother was working. Her mother had covered up the abuse, and she strictly rejected the faith of her own mother and of Conny.

We fixed a counselling session for the same evening, with both of us and with Conny. She was full of anger when she told us the story of her relative who sent her siblings away so he could abuse her. She had felt so helpless. The Holy Spirit gave us the impression that Heinrich shall ask her for forgiveness, in place of her relative. Conny agreed. After she had shouted all her pain and her anger into Heinrich's face, she was able to forgive her relative. Hildegard adjudicated him forgiveness and placed Conny in the state of virginity (that she now had again in God's eyes).

"Phew, the first backpack is gone – but the second one is even heavier", Conny said after the blessing. We did not quite understand, but we fixed a second counselling session for the next day.

The second backpack was the fact that Conny's mother knew about the abuse but covered it up in order to keep up appearances. This made Conny absolutely defenceless – because her grandmother had died in the meantime, she had nobody she could confide in.

The Holy Spirit advised us to use the representative confession of guilt again. This time, Hildegard confessed the guilt in place of the mother and asked for forgiveness. Conny shouted out her anger and despair, but she was not able to forgive. Hildegard said: "You can only do that with the power of the Spirit." We then prayed quietly in tongues and noticed a bit later that Conny was resting in the Spirit.

While resting in the Spirit, Conny said with the voice of a little girl: „Jesus says: I can forgive your mother. Therefore, I can forgive, too." Then she said in her normal voice: "Everything is going to be alright."

Then she woke again and asked: „What did I say?" We told her, and she said that she had seen Jesus approach her. She could describe him, wearing a long, white, lucent robe. He had kindly looked at her and had told her: "I can forgive your mother, and I have forgiven your mother. Then, you can do it, too." Now, she was able to forgive her mother. The second backpack had vanished, too.

This was the strongest confirmation we have ever been given by Jesus that the representative confession of guilt is important and has a wide scope that we cannot even grasp.

Sometime later, Conny sent us two e-mails:

1. How am I doing? I am doing just fine, I have not been so well in a long time, and I can tell you that I am a new person. Even my husband told me a few hours after my return that I seem a lot more balanced and friendly than before the weekend. And it is great that this effect has not ceased – and it shall not cease.
My colleagues at work are almost crazy about my new inner calmness, but in a positive sense. One of my colleagues has many problems and she would like to have some of my "good luck". I told

her that she needs to trust in God and pray, like I do. But in case of some problems, we really need to ask for help and advice, even though that may not be easy. I also had to wait for God's hints…

2. Last week, I had a wonderful dream that made me even more peaceful. I have seen my grandmother waving at me and telling me that everything is alright. She told me that she knew about it all the time, but that she did not talk to me about it out of respect. But she is happy that I have kept my love for the Father and that I got baptized, even though my mother did not like it. I had to cry and I asked our Heavenly Father to take good care of my grandmother. But I know that she is well where she is right now.
My husband is currently more interested in God. It looks like my experiences have shown him that there might be something real …

Going back into the past

Time is not a problem for God. The Holy Spirit stands above time and space.
There are two approaches to "go back into the past", i.e., to look back on and reappraise something that happened in the past:

Sometimes, the Holy Spirit asks us to go back to a certain situation in the life of the seeking person. Together with Jesus or God the Father the situation can then be experienced again, and the Holy Spirit can show something that happened but that the seeking person did not see or does not remember. This approach can be hard on the seeking person, but it might also have a relieving effect; in any case God's peace will come into the situation. Depending on what the Holy Spirit shows, forgiveness or the cancellation of a bond/curse can take place.
In trauma pedagogic, the re-experiencing of a situation is called "re-processing" (but it takes place under the guidance of a therapist, not under the guidance of the Holy Spirit).

The other approach is unusual: The Holy Spirit can instruct us to go back in time and to change something or to revise a certain situation. This sounds impossible, because in general this only happens in science fiction books or in movies.

But why should anything be impossible for the Holy Spirit?

Example:
The unforgotten wife

Conrad's wife Claire had died several years ago and had left two children. Already during her illness, Claire arranged for the time after her death: Her girl-friend Laura was to assume her role. Claire spoke with her husband and with Laura; all of them were Christians and they agreed.

Claire died, and some time later Conrad and Laura got married. Laura was a good mother to the children and tried to be a good wife to Conrad – but the first wife, Claire, somehow stood between them. Was it wrong that Conrad married the friend of his first wife? Or was it normal that Conrad could not forget his first wife?

During a counselling session we asked the Holy Spirit what to do. The word "mourning" appeared, and we asked Conrad: "Are you still in mourning for your first wife?"
"Not really. Since we got married, Laura is a wonderful wife and mother to the children, and I have bade farewell to Claire. Furthermore, I have participated in a mourning seminar."
"What happened?"
"I carried Claire through a desert until we reached the river Styx. There, I handed her to the ferryman and bade her farewell. The ferryman then rowed away and took her to the realm of the dead."

I had the spontaneous thought: "Would Claire have liked that?"
"I don't know, but I could not help it, I was in mourning."
„I think we should go and get her back, and bring her into the arms of the Father."
"Is that possible?"
Of course, it is possible, especially when the Holy Spirit wants us to do that.

In prayer, we walked through a desert and barren landscapes until we reached the river Styx. The ferryman was very surprised because we did not carry a dead person. We asked him to give Conrad's wife back. After some seesaw discussions, we ordered the ferryman in the name of Jesus to bring Claire back. He was then willing to do so and brought her back. Still in prayer, Conrad carried her all the way back, laid her in the arms of the Father and said: "This is where you belong."

Then, peace came into Conrad's heart and he knew that this was the only right place for his deceased wife.

Incidents

In this chapter, we will give an account of further incidents and examples that we have experienced. These incidents shall be perceived under the angle of diversity and variety of how the Holy Spirit acts.

We do not take credit for any of these incidents, but we are happy that God helps and acts in so many different and multifaceted ways.

God helps because he loves his children, and he intervenes in their lives.

Benjamin

Maria was already in her late thirties and single. But she had received a promise from God many years ago that she would have a son named Benjamin.

Finally, she found a partner via the Internet. He was divorced, and they married. After the marriage, she was looking forward to delivering the promised son. But she had several miscarriages. Maria and her husband were desperate when they came to see us.

The Holy Spirit showed us first that the guilt of the husband in the divorce needed to be confessed and forgiven. This happened.

Then we asked God about the couple's desire to have children. Something seemed wrong. The Holy Spirit advised us to ask for determinations. Finally, Maria spluttered: "My womb is a children's tomb." The many miscarriages had made her brittle, in spite of God's promises.

We then proclaimed God's words of truth over Maria: "This is a lie from Satan. Your womb is a place from which God will generate a child. We refuse this determination and we proclaim that your womb is a place where a child of God will be hatched."

One year later Benjamin was born.

The tree in the garden of the Father

Elizabeth had major problems accepting herself and came to see us during a hearing blessing hour during a seminar. She was not exactly attractive on the outside, and at home she was refused because she was the last of several siblings, and her father had wanted boys, not another girl.

We asked the Holy Spirit what to do. "Lay her in the arms of the Father." That was all we heard. So we prayed for her and wished her a good night.

The next morning she came to see us, was totally changed and joy was shining on her face. "Just imagine what I have dreamt tonight. Abba came and took my hand and walked with me through all my life, through all the painful experiences in my adolescence, my childhood and when I was a baby. Even back into my mother's womb during pregnancy, up to the moment of conception.

Abba said to me: 'When you were conceived, I have planted a tree in My garden, only for you and for Me, for both of us. Every time you want to, you can come and we will sit under the tree and talk to each other. I will show you my love.' "

The whale or another story of Jonah

We went to visit Helena, a friend or ours, and told her about our experiences in hearing counselling. This led her to tell us what she had on her heart.

At the end of World War II, her grandmother, her aunt and the 2-year-old daughter had cut open their wrists because they were so afraid of the approaching Russian army. The grandmother and the aunt survived, but the child died.

We asked for forgiveness in place of the grandmother and the aunt and eliminated this family guilt from Helena's life. Then, we laid (in prayer) the little girl who had died into the arms of the Father.

Then, Helena was able to tell us of another burden in her life. Her husband had cheated on her; thereupon his company sent him abroad. Helena could not remember that her husband had ever asked her for forgiveness.

In place of her husband, Heinrich asked Jesus and Helena for forgiveness, and Hildegard did the same for the former mistress of the husband. Helena then reported that she had attempted suicide during that time. She confessed that guilt, and Jesus forgave her.

At night, Helena had a dream. One remark of real life: Before Helena and her husband had moved abroad, a befriended family had given them a clay whale in whose belly the four family members were pictured.

In this dream, Helena saw an open door to a balcony, and a man stood at the balcony rail. He went from the balcony into the house, took the clay whale, went back to the balcony, climbed over the rail and disappeared. This was the moment when Helena woke up. She knew that Jesus had given her an important message with this dream: An angel came (or even Jesus himself) and took all the guilt and all the pain related to the above-mentioned incidents out of her life.

Helena was set free. Everything was alright.

The belt

Martina came to see us because she felt an inner unrest and the pressure to perform at all times. She had too much email communication (500 private emails in only two months), and she had remorses due to her marriage with a divorced man, Eric.

At first, Hildegard led the counselling session alone. When she became aware that a religious spirit was there, she asked Heinrich to join, too.

We asked the Holy Spirit what to do.

At first, we took the responsibility off Martina that her mother had laid upon her for her mentally ill sister. We also took the responsibility for the sick mother off Martina that she had burdened herself with.

Heinrich had the impression that we shall confess the guilt of the broken marriage in place of her husband, and we did so for Eric and for his former wife. Heinrich had the impulse to declare the divorced marriage as null and void. Then, we were able to bless the marriage of Martina and Eric.

Hildegard had the impression of a river with a dark current on the ground that came up to the surface. This was the religious spirit. But we did not know what its claim to Martina was. But before, she had mentioned that she wanted to gain her right to live with good performance and successes. This was the lie, and the spirit was cast out. This was confirmed by Martina's coughing, and furthermore, Heinrich smelled something burnt.

A third confirmation was given by a picture that Hildegard had: Martina had a belt tied around her waist, on which several heavy bags hang. Jesus took them off, one after the other, until only one remained. When the religious spirit was cast out, the last bag was gone, too.

Martina was free – and set free to grow in her marriage.

Shaking and Gripping

Richard and his wife came to see us for a counselling session. His mother had told him that his first year as a baby was filled with illnesses and hospital stays. He was born early after only 8 months and his mother was unable to breastfeed him due to an illness. The baby food he received caused nutritional disturbances, and two-day-old Richard was brought back into hospital. The mother was only allowed to see him through a window and was not allowed to touch him. A young doctor said: "He will have a hard time all of his life."

When Richard was a young boy he visited his grandfather who used to say: "You will never learn to speak.", and indeed, Richard only learned to speak when he was three years old. At that age, he had to go to a long medical treatment in another city. He was homesick but the doctor did not allow him to go home.

We asked the Holy Spirit for guidance. Heinrich asked Richard for forgiveness in place of the young doctor and for the grandfather. After some effort, Richard granted forgiveness and held Heinrich's hands. Immediately afterwards, Richard rested in the spirit. He kept holding Heinrich's hands and pressed them tightly while his whole body started shaking. Then Richard rested again. The shaking and resting occurred twice more. When Richard woke again he had the impression that all of Heaven cried because "we do not grip tightly", meaning that we do not hold on tightly to God's love and guidance. He had heard that and started to grip tightly.

Richard's wife had the impression that all of Heaven cried because of the horrible things that happened to Richard. We proclaimed new life over Richard. And his wife had two songs on her mind: "Come, breathe, you shall live" and a lullaby "Sleep, baby, sleep".

Hildegard had a picture: Richard was in the throne room of the Father and rested in his arms. Jesus and the Holy Spirit were around him, and the Holy Spirit breathed through his body. He breathed the power and the love of the Heavenly Father into every single body and nerve cell of Richard. The Father had wanted and protected him.

What had happened when Richard was shaking and gripping had set him free so he could step into his calling.

The big hall

Gillian had the impression that she was somehow stuck in life. When we listened to the Holy Spirit there was a very precise picture of a large, dark panelled hall, and many paintings of ancestors hung there. In the center of the hall there was a long conference table with uncomfortable chairs with high backrests. In the front part of the hall there were two large terrace doors leading into a beautiful vast garden, bathed in sunlight and with many rose bushes. There were people in the hall who did not have a single look at the garden; they were focused on the interior of the hall.

One counsellor described the picture in detail, and Gillian exclaimed: "This hall exists, just like you described. It is where the annual meeting of my extended family takes place. All come together to look back upon their glorious past."

Heinrich: "Then why don't you go outside?"
Gillian: "I cannot, these people prevent me from doing that because I belong to them."
Hildegard: "Would you like to be set free from these bonds? As a princess of the Heavenly King you belong in the luscious garden and not in the dark hall."

Gillian then dissociated herself from the bonds that tied her to her ancestors, from class conceit and pride. The Holy Spirit reminded her of details she was no longer aware of. Some people wanted to prevent

her from going outside into the garden. But in the name of Jesus they had to draw back and let Gillian outside.
Gillian was set free. The little princess was able to play and rollick in the garden of her Heavenly Father.

The pain of the Father

Teresa came to see us after Heinrich had preached about John, chapter 17, about Jesus and the Father who long to be in us. Teresa had given her life to Jesus six months before; she was divorced and had two children under the age of eight.

She suffered from this situation and cried because her children were with their father for two weeks. She suffered from being without them, even though she now had time for herself and she could have done things she would normally be unable to do.

Hildegard and Heinrich had the same impression when praying and listening to the Father – and that happens very rarely. The impression was that the Father of Jesus wanted her to have a look into his own heart, how much he grieves for his children and about those who are not with him. Teresa understood his pain and, and while she suffered because of her own children, she understood the Father and felt pity for him. She also felt that God is in her heart and carries her pain.

Gillian's answer: "It is so beautiful that the Father is in me, like you said in your sermon." She was comforted when she went away.

The white elephant

Will came to see two counsellors because he had a strange burden on his heart. He said: "I just cannot take it any longer. Not in my job, not in my family or my marriage. I am down and out, and I have bad back pains." He could not tell why.

When the counsellors listened to the Holy Spirit, a picture of a white elephant appeared. None of the counsellors could make use of it.

Only Will knew immediately what it meant: A white elephant is the present of an Indian maharaja for his worst enemy. Why? The responsibility, care and food for a white (albino) elephant – that is hardly capable of survival - require all the time and attention of the caretaker and normally exceed the financial and physical capabilities of the person who has received this present. But if the elephant dies, the wrath of the maharaja will be upon the man.

"Will, who gave you the responsibility for a white elephant? What was it that you could not bear?"
"When I was a child, my father died, and my mother gave me the responsibility for the family. I had to substitute my father although I was only six years old." That was what he could not bear.

We confessed the guilt of the mother, released Will from this responsibility and set him free. He still needs to learn to live with his newly earned freedom.

The bitter root

Mario mentioned during a counselling session that his father had committed suicide. We asked the Holy Spirit what to do.

The first picture was: A root is being extracted. One counsellor had the impression that it was a bitter root. Mario said that he had felt helpless as a fourteen year-old when his father had felt depressed and he could not help him. The Holy Spirit showed us: Mario felt responsible for the death of his father. We released Mario from the burden he had put on himself and set him free.

In a second picture, a counsellor saw how someone was retrieved out of a deep, water-filled hole. It was clear that this picture showed Mario's father; and we laid him into the arms of God the Father. The next picture was that Mario's father lay with his belly down on the lap of the Father. This picture was clear, too: When a drowned person is retrieved from the water, the water needs to flow out. We asked God for forgiveness in place of Mario's father, who had committed suicide. Then Mario's father turned on the lap of the Father (in the picture); he was alive again and looked around as if he could not believe what happened to him.

At the end, we asked Mario for forgiveness, in place of his father. Then peace came upon Mario.

40 years lost

Irene came to talk to us because she was at the end of her rope. For 40 years she had been taking counselling sessions, but not much had changed. During that time, her will and her mind were addressed, but her emotional pains did not get healed because they had happened during her childhood.

Irene had a very low self esteem and she could not overcome to depreciation and false accusations.
As a young girl, she lived with her mother at her paternal grandmother's house – her father had died in the war. For many years, she witnessed how her mother was rejected by her mother-in-law. Later, Irene herself experienced depreciation, criticizing remarks and false accusation by another relative. Furthermore, she was forced to take a job she did not like. When she got married, her mother-in-law was not happy with her because she had wished that her son would marry a "better woman".

In place of all three persons, we asked Irene for forgiveness. Irene perceived this as a restoration of her dignity. She felt how a heavy burden, that had hindered her from growing in her life with Jesus, fell off her.

Later, Irene said: "It was so different to what I had imagined. It felt so good that finally somebody asked me for forgiveness for what had been done to me."

The bet

During a conference, Alexandra came to see us for prayer because her parents had not shown her any love. She should have been a boy named Alexander, and her father was very disappointed. Even though Alexandra had the best grades at school (only A grades), her parents did not give her any appreciation.

In place of her parents, we asked Alexandra for forgiveness. We placed her in the status of a loved woman and we assured her that Abba had wanted her exactly as he had planned her and created her. Then, we blessed her for the final exams of her second degree.

The next day, Alexandra came to see us again. She had had a very bad night. A picture she had painted fell down and the wooden beams in her room crackled. Together, we went to her room to set it free from what had happened during the night. And we asked the Holy Spirit to tell us what to do. Three pictures came up:
- Backpacks were hanging on a children's coat rack in a hallway. A goat's foot stuck out of one of the backpacks.
- Some people reluctantly climbed up a snow-covered serpentine path.
- A horse-drawn sleigh.

When we had finished telling her about the pictures, Alexandra put her hands to her face. The picture of the horse sleigh had set memories free to which she had had no longer access. "They bet on me," she cried. She told us about the abuse of her school mate Marcel who was five years older. She remembered a discussion between Marcel and his friend John during a school trip on a horse sleigh. The two boys had bet with each other, and the winner was to abuse Alexandra, who was only eight years at the time. John lost and laughed.

Step by step more incidents came up. The children of her village always took a school bus to go to school. Alexandra was the only girl in the age range 6 – 10 years and the older boys teased her badly and took away her school books. Then, Marcel offered to protect her.

Before telling us about the abuse, Alexandra remembered a teacher. Miss K. did not like her and pulled her hair and dragged her through the class room. Alexandra was told: "Girls do not defend themselves".

Marcel, who had offered to protect her, then abused her. She did not defend herself. She felt so dirty that she washed herself with a strong concentrated cleansing lotion which injured her skin.

Hildegard asked Alexandra for forgiveness in place of the teacher, and Heinrich in place of the school boys.

After some tedious efforts, Alexandra was able to forgive. We had been willing to interrupt the session at any given time, but Alexandra wanted to go on. We placed her in the state of virginity that she now had again in God's eyes and we assured her that Abba would give her back what the devourer had devoured.

We then planned to cleanse the room, but the Holy Spirit drew our attention to a sentence that Alexandra had said before. At night, a voice had asked her: "Why did you forgive your parents yesterday?" This indicated that there was an unclean spirit, and this spirit was afraid to be cast out. We remembered the pictures of the backpack with the goat's foot and of the barren landscape with the people. We assumed that there were several spirits, and we asked for their names. The Holy Spirit helped us and gave us five names, one after the other. All of them had to leave.

We cleansed the room, anointed Alexandra and sent her to bed. The next morning, she came again to see us. She had slept well. But more memories had reappeared. Another abuse had happened in a corn field, and when she was able to flee after the abuse, she saw her sister sitting at a nearby bus stop. Even though Alexandra was smeared with soil, the sister did not do anything. It seemed like her sister had observed what had happened from a safe distance.

We brought the sister's guilt to Jesus, asked for forgiveness in place of her, and Alexandra forgave her.

The next day, Alexandra approached us with her bible in her hand. The Holy Spirit had drawn her attention to passages in the book of Joel, and her whole story was written there:

Joel 2, 20	Casting out spirits (the "northern horde")
Joel 2, 23	Renewed blessing like previously (abundant rains, as before)
Joel 2, 25	I will repay you (for the years the locusts have eaten)
Joel 3, 3	The bet (they cast lots for my people)

It is impressive what Abba does.

After the seminar, Alexandra wrote an email to us: When she was driving home, the streets of her village were almost empty, but she saw her former teacher, Miss K., with her husband. She had only seen her twice in the last 20 years. Alexandra did not feel any anger or rage toward her, not at all; she was even able to bless her.

The Bird

We prayed for John.
Three pictures came to our mind:
1. A dry bamboo or cane wood, but suddenly new green shots came forth.
2. A triangle, but it wasn't God, Jesus and the Holy Spirit.
3. In his soul is a black package. A bird with grey feathers and black wings is sitting on top of that package. Then a golden chain came to be put around the black package, when closed, the chain's color changed to black. Something bad happened in your childhood, which hurt your heart and soul. The bird is watching that the secrets remain hidden in you.
The chain is hindering the Holy Spirit to come to that package. The bird sitting on the package was sad.
But it was not allowing the package to be removed.

Picture one is the future, picture 2 and 3 are the same three evil things: Bird, package and chain.

Issue to be tackled first:
The Holy Spirit showed that somebody spoke powerful words to John; at the beginning they seemed to be good, but in the end, they were evil. They hurt his soul and heart.
Heinz asked Jesus acting for this person for forgiveness and broke the influence of these words on John.
The chain broke. The entitlement for the evil had been removed now.

The Holy Spirit said: **This was his father, who had spoken evil things to him**. We asked John when this happened. He said: Maybe when my parents got divorced, I was about 5 years.
Then the Holy Spirit said: there is nothing evil inside the package, it has only been declared evil. There is something very good inside, something God-given: **John's feelings and emotions**. They have been declared evil by his father.

The bird stepped down very sad now.
We declared John's emotions and feelings as gifts of God which had already being planted in him before the foundation of the world. We explained to John that this might not be easy for him to start dealing with emotions at his age of about 50. But the Holy Spirit would help him. John allowed them to come to life.

The Holy Spirit said: **The bird is his stepmother**.
The bird was sad because it realized, its time has come to an end.
We declared all connections and relationship with her to be nailed now to the cross of Jesus Christ. All ropes were cut. The entitlement has been erased, so no witchcraft is able to attack John any more.
John declared the relationship has come to an end.

The triangle now was in the sky, shining bright: Father, Son and Holy Spirit.

Unfortunately in the following time, John did not continue to separate from his past, so the progress came to a stop.

Resting in the spirit

After a church service, Ralph came to be blessed. Initially, he had not wanted to attend the service, but "something" urged him to come.

Together, we listened to the Holy Spirit. Both of us, Hildegard and Heinrich, had received impressions. When we wanted to tell Ralph about them, we noticed that he was resting in the Spirit while standing. He was swaying for some time, and then he fell backwards (we held him and put him down).

After some time, he woke again, but he could not get up. Shortly afterwards, he was resting in the Spirit again. He woke again, and then rested once more in the Spirit.

Finally, Ralph told us something, but he was not able to tell us the scope of what he had experienced. He had met Jesus and had spoken with him. But he could not tell what they had talked about. But one thing was as clear as day: Ralph now knows for sure that Jesus exists.

Epilogue

What can we say at the end of this book?
Thank you.

Thanks to the Holy Spirit who has never left or abandoned us, even when we were walking on thin ice, while holding his hand. He has always helped us: when we did not have any experience, when we did not know how to proceed, when strong emotions came up, when no human being knew what happened or what the situation was about, what the name of a spirit was… He knew it and entrusted us with his knowledge. It is a special privilege to witness the Holy Spirit acting out of the invisible into the visible world.

Thanks to Jesus, because if he had not come to earth, then the foundation for this form of counselling and hearing could not take place. Thanks that he went back to the Father and that he sent us the helper, the counsellor, the advisor, the advocate. Jesus also needed the Holy Spirit when he was on earth, as the story of his baptism by John the Baptist shows.

Thanks to God the Father, to Abba, like Jesus calls him and like we may call him, too. The everlasting love of the Father for his children sometimes overflows us in a way that we can only cry. The Father cannot be without his children; his mercy tears within him. Sometimes, we are able to have a look at his heart. And this is, literally, touching and smashing.

Thanks to all people who put their trust in us. Of course, not everything was healed and well in their lives after a counselling session. But important steps in their lives were taken, and more are to follow. We will work on that with the Holy Spirit until the end of our lives.

Thanks to our friends who supported and encouraged us, who proofread and gave advice: Peter and Ursel Wichmann, Wolfgang and Angela Bienert, Michael and Conny Adler and our daughter Kerstin Becker. And Susan Schuelke, who finalized the translation.

We might summarize this whole book into one core sentence:

As long as the Holy Spirit guides us we do not need to know what to do when counselling.

Heinrich and Hildegard Becker
June 2013

Biographical Information

Heinrich Becker
- Degree in Mathematics and Business Administration in Technical University of Berlin.
- Until 2009 Executive Manager in major multinational corporations in the area of logistics.
- Speaker on many national and international logistics conferences.
- Co-author of "Handbuch Kommissionierung" (compendium order picking) Heinrich Vogel Verlag, Munich 2009.
- Since 1970 voluntary work in a Christian network with focus on counselling.
- Speaker and preacher in several churches.

Hildegard Becker
- Degree as teacher for elementary and secondary school, followed by 10 years of teaching.
- Leader of "Breakfast for Women" in Frankfurt/Germany in the mid 1980ies (www.fruehstueckstreffen.de).
- After job-related move of the husband leader of "Breakfast for Women" in Munich until 2009.
- Since 1970 voluntary work in a Christian network with focus on counselling.
- Speaker at many "Breakfast for Women" events in Germany, Austria and Switzerland.
- Preacher in several churches.
- Author of „Die Lebensmitte kommt bestimmt" (Midlife comes for sure), Johannis Verlag, 1999.

Notice

Notice

Also available in German:

BoD – Books on Demand 2013
Norderstedt, Germany
ISBN978-3-3-8482-6660-9